KT-369-876

TRUE NORTH

© *Bokförlaget Max Ström 2004*
Text: Tommy Hammarström and Per Wästberg 2001. © *Photographs: Property of the Photographers*
Picture Editor: Jeppe Wikström. Picture Research: Stefan Borgius. Captions: Tommy Hammarström
Translation: Kim Loughran. Design: Patric Leo. Layout: Mikael Jacobsson
Colour Separation and Printing: Fälth & Hässler, Värnamo, Sweden, 2004
Binding: Fälth & Hässler, Farsta, Sweden
Third Impression

Printed on Arctic matt 170 gsm and Munken Lynx 150 gsm from Trebruk, Sweden

ISBN 91-89204-26-3

TRUE NORTH

The Grand Landscapes of Sweden

TEXT TOMMY HAMMARSTRÖM AND PER WÄSTBERG

PRINCIPAL PHOTOGRAPHER TORE HAGMAN

CONTENTS

Sweden is a clearing in the forest, a glade among the firs. From the beginning it was no more than that — a large country with a thinly dispersed population, huge distances between the farms, huge distances between people.

Mostly, there were trees. More than half the country is still forest: coniferous forest, birch forest, alder forest, oak forest and beech forest. The coast is lined with a hundred thousand rocky islands; the rest is lakes, bogs, marshes, tundra and mountains. In small gaps and clearings, people built their kingdoms; tilled land is only a fraction of the land area and built–up land an even smaller part.

Which gives Swedes a particular feeling for forests — they have lived in them almost forever. Now, nearly everyone lives in towns and conurbations, far from the forest. But the feeling remains. Ask people how they see paradise and most will still think of that gap between the trees, the clearing, and of forests.

Sweden is a forest realm, and its modern society grew from within the forest. This is a paradox. Timber and pulp were the underpinning of welfare, as were the veins of ore through the hills. And in clearings people built the widely promulgated Swedish Model. The poor, backward forestland of the north, a sub-Arctic outpost in Europe, was the richest and the most equitable. And for half a century it was so. Spared war and revolutions for almost two hundred years, the people built a kingdom of the golden mean, the most modern of nations. A strong and benign state managed and dispensed welfare. It was measured out in portions and at a rate uniquely Swedish, of which we are proud.

The Swedish model has been transformed. Sweden is no longer unparalleled. The once-lauded system is changed and defiled. And we are no longer an outpost, we are no longer solitary forestland. More than ever, we are part of the wider world. As many people as emigrated to America in our time of adversity now immigrate to Sweden in this time of welfare. And an especially homogenous land has become a multi-cultural society. Every tenth Swede has first-generation roots in another country and another environment, and outside the forest grow other landscapes and other feelings.

Sweden is an urbane, continental state, very much a part of Europe. It has come to this — the forest people have become city dwellers. A thinly spread population has accumulated into large cities; three of the country's nine million live in the three largest cities and nearly all the rest live in smaller cities, along the coast or in cultivated landscape.

But the forest remains, the landscape, all of Nature. Over beyond, the ridges mist into blue, the lakes glint, the firs darken, the clearings lighten. There is Sweden. There is our true north.

Tommy Hammarström   Per Wästberg

The roads curve white and narrow across the coastal landscape. The air is as luke-
warm as the water in the rain barrel. A buzzard hangs poised in the air over its hidden
prey. The island dells are filled, in their southern aspect, with blossoming snowball-
trees, swallow-wort and crimson crane's bill. Swans float on the water like heavy
bookmarks. At midsummer, the butterfly orchis sends its scent of passion across the
outlying islets. The dusk shifts mirage-like granite islands to beyond the horizon. Boats
sway silent in the sea mist. Reality has cut its moorings. We are gutting perch and pike.
Talk is unobtrusive. A cuckoo in the west proclaims the waning of summer. We are
in a calm on the ocean bay, with ethereal islets, drifting eider ducks, and sandpiper
song for dinner. We are sailing in silence, with no specific destination, arriving when
the wind lets us, anchoring in the rain, surrendering to the cool of evening, to silence
and reading.

The scene changes: a strong breeze, thunder and threatening cobalt blue waters —
and sudden wafts of warmth between desolate points. We cast off at first grey light
with the air redolent of loneliness and the seagulls silent. Somewhere, leaves are being
burned; there's a fire taste nudging at my palate. Winter days are yet distant, when
swirled snow covers bald skerries and the new moon is cradle-rocked in the treetops.

The crab-apples are shimmering balls in the dark leaves. The ferns stand tall, the
hairy willow herb is blooming late in wet spaces. A spider tightens its circle around
the web. The clutches of rowanberries are on fire in October. Our wake glistens with
stars. In the archipelago's early winter, tansy pokes up through the snowdrifts. Flocks
of wintering long-tailed ducks drift between the combs of the waves. The moorings on
the jetty are iced stiff.

A hard southwesterly lifts ice floes and stacks them, as they bellow and snarl like bucks mating, cracks splitting through them like lightning. Salmon anglers who have parked on the shore and continued out over the ice on kick-sleds to their patches of water, hasten back to shore. The end of April is nettle picking time, the cuckoo calls from the east and wild ducks hurry in swift lines under a glue-white sky. In May, the islets float like bales of leaves, swallows hunt their insects and man, his hand on the rudder, chases time, more time. The littoral year has run full cycle.

As the seagull flies, Sweden's coast is approximately 2,500 kilometres long, but for the sailor who has to enter and exit bays and gaps, the true length is a large multiple of that. The archipelagic landscape is among the rarest of coastal formations. For hundreds of thousands of years, glacial ice has been polishing the rock and sculpting the roundest of shapes. The ice's movement is reflected in furrows that look freshly made. Waves and surf have rinsed clean the rocks and made them legible as in few other places on earth. There is a mild look to the southern Swedish coast with its deciduous trees, clumps of reeds, fields, stone mounds and stretches of meadow. The nightingale and sedge-warbler sing in the birch leaves, through the hum of the Baltic Sea, along the bays and hillsides of the coast of Blekinge province, to the southwest.

The southernmost provinces of Skåne and Halland are the only ones without archipelagos. On Skåne's coastal meadows, shaped by perennial grazing along The Sound between Sweden and Denmark, thick grass tussocks reach almost down to the waterline. The wind-blown sand of the Halland coast is held down by grass and pine. Lyme-grass follows the long, grey, rubble-strewn beaches. Here, the earth meets the sea, with no islands in between, in a dramatic transformation where stone and grains of sand have ground at each other for millions of years.

The harbours are mostly man-made; north of Varberg, the coastline rises and forms bays with protected anchorages. The valleys and plains are fertile and the old towns have their origins in fishing villages and ineffectual defence posts. On the heaths, broom flowers in June, briar in July, bell-heather in August. In the old days, the heaths were burned off to rejuvenate the heather and keep juniper trees at bay.

The coast has been worked hard by farming; patches of natural growth are few. Untouched are only the coastline strips with their seaweed and algae ramparts, red-grey cliffs and pastures for horses and heifers. Rose hip grows here, and spindle-tree and blackberry; wild oats sway, and the wind has forced the deciduous trees into knotty resistance. Stonecrop and thyme, their gold and violet so closely akin to the country's flag colours that they become the insignia of the Swedish coast.

Bjärehalvön Peninsula and Kullen were the first areas in Sweden to thaw out from under the glacial ice — six thousand years ago. The land stepped up from the sea, mire became meadow and meadows became countryside. Sketched against the horizon are the hill of Kullaberg with its lighthouse, Hovs hallar with its reddish hillsides and, riding at anchor out on the Kattegatt Straits, the island of Hallands Väderö.

The island has been given environmental protection status, and Stone Age hunters would still be familiar with the swamp hollows and sacrificial groves and the intimidating root system of the alder, with hawthorn and snowball-trees between its toes. There are sombre crypts of ivy, an alder copse in wet ground with sword lilies shining poisonously and heavy ferns billowing to the song of the nightingale. Jungly deciduous forests like this once dominated Sweden's open plains.

The coastal flora of Bohuslän province to the southwest is spartan, its cliffs polished by sea and glacier. The glaciers that produced flat surfaces on northern aspects retreated twelve thousand years ago. The trees are wind-bent and salted from the storms that reach several kilometres inland. The humid westerly winds press the deciduous trees up against the valley walls. Rugged grey cliffs rise, seemingly naked, over water which turns the colour scale to blue. The sea smells of salt and rotten beds of seaweed, wild honey-suckle clings to the coastal ravines, while the waves bash like weapons in a period film.

Along garden paths and in graveyards there are shells, smooth or spiky, whispering from sea-depths where many coastal people have remained. On other graves there are net buoys and glass floats. Cargo ships, these days without funnels, glide along the horizon. Never again will we read the graphic messages of ship smoke against the sky.

Narrow meadows crowd into Bohuslän's notched valleys between massive rocky walls: daisies, burnet saxifrage, red clover. There is a scent of sea and lilacs on the wind, loneliness and idyll. The hidden ravines and the dangerous sea are more the signature of the west coast than the Baltic coast.

In this Gulf Stream climate, rocks store the heat of the sun. Here, the sea is at its most salty, the vegetation Northern Atlantic; southern trees like the beech thrive, as do mountain flora such as dwarf birch. Less common are cowslip and blue anemone, the flowers of the east coast.

There are archipelagos in the southwest and almost all the way up the east coast to Haparanda in the far north. The archipelagic sea north of Stockholm is a swarm of skerries, thinning out towards the Åland Sea. Approaching the archipelagos from the outside, the islands seem anonymously similar, rocky tops that merge and lean towards a horizon of dark forest and indefinite cliff shapes — not an appealing landscape, rather a domain dominated by dangerous reefs and treacherous passages.

There is little untouched nature left in Sweden except for a few outer skerries, bogs and swamps and the mountain slopes of the north. Near the Finnish border up north, we find an archipelago more melancholic and uninhabited than those to the south. It consists of moraine: sand, gravel and rubble. Swampy ground links coastline and heath. The flora has migrated from the Arctic Ocean coast: arctic wormwood and blue fields of beach pea. The September sky arches rock-grey over wind-whipped pines along the shores. In crevices and depressions, dwarf birch run flame-coloured; grasping each other in the wind's relay race. Along the coast of Västerbotten province, birches stand, silvery supernatural, close to the low coastal meadows. To the south comes the herring coast, and close by its steep slopes, the scent of bog bilberry and sweet gale spreads over still marsh waters and springy quagmire.

In Ångermanland province, the Swedish coast is at its steepest and most inaccessible. Forested hills topple three hundred metres to the sea. There are hidden water-lily ponds, ridges along the horizon, silvery barns and white vicarages. At Ullångerfjärden Bay and Skuleberget Mountain, land and sea meet dramatically. The granite falls abruptly and the bay meanders inland.

Much further south, in the archipelagos of Kalmarsund and Tjust, old rock and mid-European deciduous forest alternate. Nightingales sing and great crested glebes sail by reedy, serpentine shores. Sloping meadows of meadow saxifrage tip down towards the Baltic. In his novel, *By the Open Sea*, August Strindberg sees the Baltic as a great loneliness with rough waters, ambushing winds and taciturn people drying their nets. And an isolation that stretches from Söderarm down to the unapproachable Blå Jungfrun.

Outside important coastal cities such as Gothenburg, Norrköping, Sundsvall and Härnösand, cultivated landscape secedes to wilderness. Despite a growing population, there is an abundance of deserted coastal strips and uninhabited islands. Seaside vegetation is meagre: sea starwort, scentless mayweed and higher up, wild pansy and yellow stonecrop. The cliffs are dark with crusty lichen where waves wash over; above, the lichen is orange and greenish-yellow. In May, black-throated divers on their way from the Black Sea to the White dip over the outer bays and the sweetly polished ancient rocks of Svenska Högarna. Tens of thousands of small birds, escaping the Arctic coast, navigate by these beacons.

The two largest islands in the Baltic Sea are Gotland and Öland: they are also Swedish provinces, their essences marked by the battle against the sea on every side. They are barren but comely: in our time, they have become summer resorts dependent on tourism. When Carl Linnaeus landed on Öland Island in June 1741, he was rejoicing in life: "The road led through the most enchanting groves one has seen, which greatly exceeded in beauty every place in Sweden and could compete with all in Europe. They comprised linden trees, hazels and oak with flat, green soil with neither stone nor moss. Here and there, one glimpsed the most beauteous fields. For one who has tired of this world's unstable temperament and seeks to escape its vanity to tranquil obscurity, there can be no more pleasant retreat."

The lighthouses and points at Falsterbo, Ottenby and Grötlingboudd are staging posts for migratory birds to rest and get their bearings in April and September on the route between the Arctic Ocean coast and Senegal, Congo and the Cape. It is extraordinary to see a flock of small waders descend on an open beach, position themselves with their chests all in the same direction, tuck heads under wings, and lift up one leg for a couple of hours of sleep, followed by a bath and a preen, then away.

The long coastline of Öland Island fades in the sunset. Wind-blown junipers, junipers camouflaged as cypresses — disguised, they spread. Öland's great limestone plain is, at its most rugged, a Nordic steppe with thinly spaced tussocks, gravel on smooth limestone rocks, small herbs burned by the sun. What remains are lichens and other hardies. In May, larks ring out like glass bells over the boulders. The monotonous warning of oyster-catchers mixes with the low whistle of the golden plover. Öland's toads and grasshoppers belong on the southern Russian steppes; for many reptiles and insects, Öland is a western outpost.

The rock-roses bloom pale yellow on the great plain at the end of May. Pollen remains indicate that it was here at the end of the Ice Age. It also grew in central Europe at that time; now the species has become extinct everywhere but here.

The great plain was not formed by nature, but by sheep grazing and centuries of tree-felling to feed the lime ovens. If grazing were stopped, low-growing pine and birch would take over. The sky over the great plain is a huge tent, tied down by the white church steeples. Today, the plain entrances you by its nakedness, freed from irrelevance: earth and sky, harsh winters, glorious light in summer.

The Segerstad lighthouse rises above the plain with its low stone walls. Die-straight farm lanes to the sea, grey sheep with black heads. We rest on roughly grazed grass among tansy and thistle, quaking-grass and hairgrass. At a distance from one of the farms, hammer blows are heard. In the morning clanging of a church, larks bounce in silence over their nests.

In September, the sea is strangely still under the searching green eye of the lighthouse. Flocks of eiders move out to sea where a small boat with dark sails like a pirate ship beats northward. A ploughshare of wild geese reaches toward the Long Jan lighthouse and further towards Travemünde, Marseille …

It is time for blackberries to ripen, the bindweed rings blustery blue in roadside ditches, pale Michaelmas daisies poke up around the kitchen steps and bunches of wormwood are thrown into the firewood bin. Grey farmhouses are like small fortresses behind walls with knotted apple trees, thickets of plums and sour cherries. The yet unharvested barley's feelers sway like thin mist. In a pasture, delphiniums and white sweet peas protrude from a vanished farmstead.

The island is at its narrowest at Föra Church. In the churchyard lies the priest Martinus, murdered by a bailiff; there are sea pilots and spiced-bread bakers, vicars and their wives, and a nameless young servant girl with many children who died.

In September, dragonflies with Prussian blue wings swish over the cemetery walls, landing, trembling, one final time. Forget-me-nots bloom again, but the sea starwort has gone to seed. Summer calls on autumn for help in covering its tracks. Asp and rowan redden, lingonberries darken. Curlews take off from between tussocks. The great plain turns the grey of worn sails.

On Gotland Island, the great *raukar*, or pillar formations, were shaped by the breaking waves of the Littorina Sea about 65,000 years ago. Embankments of boulders and the *raukar* indicate the level of the Littorina Sea, fifteen metres above the present sea level. Shale lies in the sand like flat coins. Dried seaweed crunches under our feet. In the fields are mounds from the Bronze Age; sheep have cropped their pates.

From the limestone floor grows blueweed, giving Gotland a colour shade as typical as Öland's sparkling rock-rose. Soil collects in cracks in the island's limestone spine, hiding the Solomon's seal and crimson crane's bill and giving a foothold to sloe, hawthorn and rose-hip. The marshes that remain attract wild ducks and curlews to their shallow, toad-rich mud. Stone walls, the *vastar*, mark the boundaries between worked fields and thin grazing land. Proud parasol mushrooms rig up their shades; in a couple of days, the underside will have darkened. Mullein stretches up from sun-warmed cracks in the limestone. Close by is the heath with quarry shafts, isolated houses with cows and sheep and the island's southernmost tip, Hoburgen Point, in the sea. Swedish whitebeam trees along the ridges have been twisted by the winds, their roots and branches like crooked toes and fingers. There is a smell of moss and fungi, with a sharpness to the fermentation that forebodes winter and cold.

Cairns have been stacked here over the centuries. Fields became overgrown when entire villages emigrated to America, died of cholera (in 1864) or starved to death (1868). Walking alone here, it seems as though you are in company anyway, with hay-makers, shepherds, farm-hands, cattle-tenders, women milking and girls raking.

In King Karl xiv Johan's time, one tenth of Gotland was swampland, a mixture of marsh and shallow lakes. The great marshes, like Line Marsh near Roma, with their fields of saw grass, rare relics of a warmer Europe; destructive draining has widely encroached. In 1833, a census was taken of all the fully grown oaks on Gotland; there were 258,000. There are few left, even though boats are now built of armour plate and plastic. When land redistribution came to Sweden, revolutionising agriculture, forested meadows on common land suffered, the land being owned by village communities and co-operatives. Land redistribution spread people out to isolated farmsteads. Most forested meadows were divided up and became farmed fields. The wide branches and broad treetops of the old oaks indicate that they did not grow in forests but rather on open, common land, in pastures and hayfields.

Gotland's pastures are not transformed deciduous forests but former farmland that reverted to managed forest in poorer times, with clearings kept open for hay-making and grazing and windfall wood collected for fuel. Forest meadows are the result of co-operation between man and nature.

In May and June, sloe and dewberry bloom. Eyes down, roads creep through white caves of birdsong. From the limy soil grow orchids like nowhere else in Sweden: early purple orchids and the rare *orchis spitzelii* under shady bushes on land grazed by sheep. They may be remnants from a period of warmer weather. Species crossbreed here, producing hybrids; nature reappearing in new disguises.

The Stockholm archipelago is the opposite of Öland and Gotland: here, a formidable giant, reeling with vertigo, has slung twenty-four thousand islets in a wide arc eastward from the capital. It is fifty kilometres from the resort of Furusund in the north to the outermost skerries. The archipelago sea consists of groups of islands and for the dedicated explorer, each of them is a world in itself. There is no other major city with such a wide, rich and largely unexploited area out to sea. Several rock species found in the Stockholm archipelago are reckoned to be about two billion years old. The island of Resarö with its feldspar mine at Ytterby, abandoned when it reached a depth of 150 metres, is world famous among geologists: four basic elements take their names from the island. A number of other unique minerals were first discovered here as well, among them fergusonite, which radioactively dates rock species.

From the mix of forest meadow and field in cultivated landscape, it is a short journey to the outer edge of the archipelago. The archipelago compresses the shapes of Swedish nature. In the eyes of sailors, each island is individual, but together they are a landscape risen from the sea, changing with the sea's various tonal keys.

The cliffs have been formed by wind and wave; they fall like tent sides down to water level. Apollo butterflies with their red, black-rimmed eye patches dance over sun-warmed rock spines and ice-polished slabs. Deep into autumn, mourning cloaks flap their velvet-brown, blue-dotted wings. Peacock butterflies, whose wing markings frighten insect-eating birds, pass the winter in boat-houses.

Before the days of sea charts, sailors and fisherfolk committed to memory the outline of each islet rock and merged the islands into unexpected patterns that disappeared in sea mist. New channels constantly materialise on one's route to the sea.

The old way of life in the archipelago was farming combined with fishing and navigation. This has been replaced by weekend commuting from the city; ferries and bridges have reduced the need for boats. Steamboats have re-emerged, to carry tourists on cruises in the beautiful natural surroundings of the channels, with music and dancing on board and landfalls in isolated places. In an hour, you can reach places where there have been dwellings for a thousand years but which are still unspoiled. The rough-hewn islanders who for centuries supplied Stockholm with essentials are gone. Today, not even the lighthouses are manned. In the outer archipelago, silver-grey huts stand abandoned.

Few of the islands are large enough to permit self-sufficiency. Winters were lonely; for lengthy periods, people could not leave their island. With the grim climate, sickness and taxes, it is strange that many have endured in their archipelago homes through generations. Farmed fields were few but there was pasture for the animals, and eggs, seabirds, fish and boat building. The settlement at Kudoxa, by Svartlöga Island, sustained about forty inhabitants from the 16th century until the First World War. By the 1940s, there were no permanent residents left.

Some larger islands like Svartlöga have uncontrolled, low-forest growth. Alders thick with ticks, meadow-sweet at a man's height and copious vipers make the inland of Svartlöga difficult to penetrate. But there are also crab-apples, a collapsed fence, a rusted ploughshare: signs of human presence now ceased.

Many of the island groups are in dangerous outer-skerry waters where steamboats would not venture even in summer. Electrification was never feasible. And the sea is seldom co-operative but mostly in agitation, with leeward shelter hard to find.

The flora of the outer archipelago's shore-line is typical of the Swedish coast: scentless mayweed, tansy, sea starwort, orpine, St. John's wort, wild chives. And butterfly orchis, whose root, gently boiled and crushed, will make a comatose man vigorous in bed and cause a woman to lose control — according to Carl Linnaeus.

Although the flora is fairly similar from island to island, the contours, crevices and bays are as different as the facial characteristics of relatives. The Rödlöga Storskär group, for example, has almost highland terrain with low birch, heather, crowberry, alder, ash and snowball-tree. Trees have come back to the outer islands. In the old days, they were taken for timber — for boat decks and housing frames, for bailers and clothes beaters.

There is room for everything in the changeable and inexhaustible Stockholm archipelago where I grew up. There are even uninhabited islands for people of somewhat advanced age who like playing Robinson Crusoe. Between 1860 and 1910, a summer-holiday version of Stockholm was built, with picturesque Swiss chalets, masonry palaces, gazebos and fake ruins. Well-to-do Stockholmers were escaping from the stench and noxious gases to better air — just as Gothenburgers found their way to Marstrand and Särö Island. It was summer camp for children of the rich, a water playground without the dangerous undertow. And it was to grow. These days, passenger ferries pick up and drop off at about 170 jetties and there are more than two hundred thousand summer visitors in more than fifty thousand cottages.

Once upon a time, there were summer settlements quite close to the centre of Stockholm. Along the shipping channels were villas with turrets and verandas — a patriarchal middle class smelling of liqueurs with large families, many maids and huge loads of luggage to be carted back and forth in June and August. There were bathhouses with pools slippery with seaweed, garden arbours, croquet, peas cooked in their shells, crayfish, flotillas at regatta time, *aquavit* cooling in bags trailing behind boats.

The summer islands were holiday homes for city kids. No one bothers to mark all the long winters: we are truly alive only in the holidays, as summer visitors. This is when existence gets its specific weight. This is when we are close to the elements, and smell the early summer scents of lily-of-the-valley and boat varnish, see the newly blossomed Swedish whitebeam, the tall wild chervil and the sky polished like a boat's stern. This is when lawns are dewed with daisies, purple lilacs gather by the outdoor privy, and clips with glass weights pin down tablecloths outdoors so a cordial glass will not tip under attack from the stormy bays of life. Summer holidays must not be weighty. They must hover on cliff-tops or rest lightly by the waterside like a dipper on his rock. Wind must blow through houses, the radiance changing them. Their structural elements should not be visible. Houses must want to lift like kites and sail off into the insatiable oneness of a June evening. Fret-saw work and gingerbread carpentry are apt terms for describing the villas that stand untouched, like time capsules sunk to the sea-bed, spared from war, social transformation, new habits.

Steamboat traffic in the Stockholm archipelago was busy up until the 1950s. The routes made a fine network of arteries between the islands. Each ferry on the Vaxholm run had its own steam whistle signal and its own regular customers expecting to greet the same first mate and the same gold-bedecked captain on the bridge, year after year. A bouquet of smells greeted passengers on the gangplank: engine oil, fuel wood, tar and the sizzle of fried steamboat beef and onions from the forward cabin. The noise of propellers at full-speed-reverse was the prelude to a summer of adventure, and we who lived along the route learned to identify engine sounds out on the bay, even at night, half-asleep. During the Second World War, this culture of summer fun was superseded by a trend favouring cabins further out in the archipelago: those who spent time there were not interested in renting cottages from fisherfolk or farmers, nor did they want to live as plushly as they did in town — they wanted to blend in with the landscape and not have to deal with other people as did an earlier generation. They were pioneers who travelled by outboard motorboat or speedboat.

The archipelago has become Stockholm's largest amusement park. The authorities have had to step in with regulations for shoreline-amendments, planning permission, preservation orders and purchases of island groups to conserve a singular water-world for posterity. Perhaps Sweden is unique in so developing summer vacationing to a lifestyle — with the villas of the inner Stockholm archipelago as that lifestyle's crowning glory. Neither does any other country possess the equivalent of these forested meadows rich in herbs, serpentine straits and a rock base scratched by glacier claws.

This glistening swarm of seal-grey rocks resembles a broken pearl necklace. It offers us a leaf-garlanded bosom of water, a love-child of nature so appealing that, in the words of Baudelaire, it "makes creation less common, the minutes less arduous".

Lee and storm, home and estrangement are the seaboard's contrasting poles. The whistle of the redshank cuts the silence into two sheets: sea and sky. A breathing-space is created, a joy like a long adagio. Early summer coolness over shorelines adorned with new leaves. In June, the song-thrush whistles between the islands. The sweet smell of red clover and wild chervil greets you in the morning. A buoy dips its head under the water, the anchor chain slimy. In the semi-real light of midsummer nights, white flowers gleam supernaturally, the others lose their colour.

The air is warmer over limestone islands than over granite ones; lime retains heat, raspberries ripen earlier and the vegetation is more southern European. The islands are completely different, they are not anchored but seem to move according to season and cut across each other's course. They are encapsulated in haze; your gaze picks them out, one after another. One is the secretive island, another is populated by people who fly pennants and stoke their saunas. Some are grey and aloof, others entice us with siren song and cherry sweetness. Using a flashlight, I grope through the cool grass to the earth cellar to get beer and potato *aquavit* and make my way back to the veranda between water and treeline, and as the hours progress, I too become a bridge between the wilds and cultivation. I walk down to rock slabs still warm under my soles and dive into the water, quietly, to not disturb the caddis flies and aerial insects of different kinds. There is the lightest of breezes, bringing with it a note of violet, a scent of alder trees. In the moonlight, the pine bark glows like amber; meanwhile, the sea pales and becomes as lightly brittle as tissue paper.

In early June, the limestone rocks on Öland's great plain seem to mirror the sun. Above all the yellow lapwings swivel, golden plovers call plaintively, wheatears on walls lap noisily. In a marsh, the black-tailed godwit, its breast brick-red, is coming in to land. The sea is grey-green, striped with white in the summer storm approaching Distaff Week, the late July week with calendar days dubbed, in the Swedish tradition, with given names. (This week all seven days have women's names — thus: Distaff Week. The week is said to portend rain.) Later comes August and its harebells and lady's bedstraw. The swallows now have their young and the gooseberries are yellowing. White butterflies flap over the mounds of seaweed on the leeward shores.

In September, cranes arrive, gracious, silken grey, on the fields at Ottenby to provision themselves with grasshoppers and grain spilled from harvesters. Their horn calls bring curlews and oyster-catchers in their thousands. The meadow-sweet has gone to seed but the tansy's yellow buttons glimmer as on a discarded uniform. Maiden dragonflies rustle. A cormorant stretches its lizard throat and sniffs the hatred of fisherfolk and farmers: the coastal graffiti spoiler.

I have seen shelducks, magnificently motley and heavy as geese, take off from Grötlingboudd Point and ringed plovers and dunlins comb the Baltic waves, while a pair of ospreys unite and black-headed arctic terns suggested musical notes trying to incorporate the hum, the chirping, the mewling of the buzzards.

Around the first of October, the larks move off, as do the last swallows from the islands of Öland and Gotland. Harvest chaff blows across the roads. Apples bump on to the ground in a sudden autumn storm, thrushes seizing on them immediately, and the first leaves to fall are the ash's. Centuries sweep across whitewashed limestone houses, across crown imperials and lungwort. "Families follow family paths." Time will not reverse, but the return of the seasons leaves us in comfort and awe.

A string of newly arrived spring light links the treetops. The frost lifts to become dew. Every egg that rests in an artistically woven nest is full of future birdsong.

Per Wästberg

THE LANDSORT LIGHTHOUSE (p. 21). On Öja Island at the southern entrance
to the Stockholm archipelago is the old Landsort lighthouse and pilot station.
A pilot was stationed here from 1535 and the lighthouse, built in 1678, was the first
on the east coast. The lighthouse is now completely automated, the pilot lookout
has been shut down and the number of pilots reduced. Öja's inhabitants have turned
to other professions: tourist boat rides and marine taxis, a sea rescue school and
IT — for example, the islanders handle the Employment Office switchboard calls.

MOON OVER ÅSTOL (pp. 22–23). The fishing village of Åstol Island, with its 300
inhabitants, is between Marstrand and Tjörn on the west coast. The village grew
up in the 1760s during a rich and storied herring-fishing epoch. There were grandiose
fish harvests in Bohuslän province from 1748 until 1808. The island is now a popular
summer resort, with one facility lacking — cars.

WINTER IN SKÄRHAMN VILLAGE (pp. 24–25). The old fishing village of Skärhamn
on the west side of Tjörn Island in Bohuslän has a well protected harbour — its name
means 'harbour inside the skerries'. The town has developed an economy based on cargo
handling and shipping. It is also a centre for the preparation of that ubiquitous Swedish
Christmas delicacy, *lutfisk,* or boiled ling.

ICE FORMATIONS AT BOVALLSTRAND IN BOHUSLÄN (p. 26). Winter on the
west coast is generally ice-free, but at times, coastal waters can freeze over. The water
solidifies in movement and ripples become patterns.

SPRING WARMTH IN KYRKESUND (p. 27). Houses and boathouses crowd along the
bare rock of Kyrkesund Sound, Bohuslän province, in the April sun.

SMOOTH ROCKS ON TRYGGÖ ISLAND (p. 29). Bohuslän's red granite is polished
and bare. Salt spray keeps even lichen from the rock. This granite used to be favoured for
construction work and stone-cutting workshops were dotted along the coast. In many
places, sharp, ugly sores in the rock testify to previous quarry work.

THE NEW TJÖRN BRIDGE AND A REGATTA (pp. 30—31). The annual Tjörn
Island sail race passes under the new suspension bridge linking the island with the
mainland. Almost all archipelago islands now have bridge connections to the
mainland, superseding the old ferries. This has vastly improved access: Tjörn Island
is now a comfortable commute from Gothenburg.

BARE ROCKS ON GLUPPÖ ISLAND (pp. 32—33). The Swedish coast and archipelago
along Skagerak are characterised by naked rock, appealingly glacier-polished. A third
of all coastal landscape in Bohuslän province is made up of rock like this. In many of the
clustered fishing villages there is just enough soil for vegetable patches.

A SEASIDE PINE AT HAVÄNG (p. 35). Tamed by winds and salt spray, this lonely
pine stands on a coastal meadow looking like a bonsai. Skåne has no archipelagos
and the coastline is relatively even, with no real bays. The moors at Haväng have been
used for grazing since ancient times, and sandy beaches stretch northward towards
Blekinge province.

THE TOWN OF MÖLLE, IN A WESTERLY GALE (pp. 36—37). The Kullen Peninsula juts out into The Sound between Sweden and Denmark with Kullaberg Hill as its outmost point. Mölle, nestling into the hill's southern slope, was once an important fishing harbour, landing tonnes of Baltic herring at a time when it was a staple for Skåne's dinner tables. Later, Mölle became a fashionable resort.

MORNING MIST AT KÅSEBERGA (pp. 38—39). Grassy meadows pitch steeply into the sea at Kåseberga, in Skåne province. In a protected bay at the foot of the slope is the fishing hamlet and rescue station. Up on the ridge is one of Sweden's most fascinating ancient relics, the Ale stenar Stones. This part of the country was settled in ancient times.

MALMÖ'S RIBERSBORGSBADET BEACH (p. 41) Like confetti, bathers are strewn across the white sand and sprinkled onto the shallow, cloudy water. A jetty extends out to the deeper waters of The Sound. The beach is almost in downtown Malmö, between the old Kockum shipping yard and the new Öresund Bridge.

HALL-HANGVAR NATURE RESERVE (p. 42) This fifteen kilometre-long beach at the most northwesterly reach of Gotland Island is currently a protected reserve. It is a rugged coastline, dressed with dwarfed pine, steep cliffs and stony beaches but also lush wetlands, wet meadows and rare orchids.

WIND POWER PLANTS ON GOTLAND ISLAND (p. 43). Windmills for the new age produce electricity in its cleanest form, releasing nothing but sighs to the wind. They have to be built where the wind blows hardest and for many, the coastline is spoiled by the tall, white windmills. Sweden's largest wind power park is at Näsudden Point on Gotland Island, where 94 propellers spin, five of the masts built in the sea. The electricity produced is the equivalent of a tenth of a nuclear reactor's output.

DUNES ON GOTSKA SANDÖN ISLAND (pp. 44–45). Less than forty kilometres north of Fårö Island in the Baltic Sea, a sand reef rises from the sea to form a strange island, known for dead pines, beetles and shipwrecks. Gotska Sandön Island is the most remote island in the Baltic but it has been inhabited since ancient times; in the 19th century, the population was all of 50 people. Now, only Swedish Environmental Protection agency staff live here. The entire island, including 300 metres of territorial water, is a national park.

STATELY BLUE VIPER'S BUGLOSS (pp. 46–47). These blue flowers indicate lime-rich soil. The dryness is typical of Öland Island, the province with the least rainfall in Sweden. Between the island and the mainland rises the round pate of Blå Jungfrun (the Blue Virgin), an old navigational aid and a fabled island. It is known as the mountain where witches live, travelling across the country regularly each Easter.

THE BYRUM RAUKAR UNDER SIEGE (p. 48). A *rauk* is a pillar in the sea, a stone sculpture chiselled by the sea: waves gnaw away the softer stone and leave a statue of harder minerals, often dramatically shaped. Most *raukar* — and the biggest — are found along the coast of Gotland Island, but at Byrum on the west of Öland Island, there is a 600-metre stretch of coast with a hundred or so beautifully moulded sculptures.

JUNGFRUSKÄR IN THE TJUST ARCHIPELAGO (pp. 50–51). In the archipelago off Loftahammar in north-eastern Småland, a shipping channel goes through the narrow straits at Jungfruskär, cheek by jowl with summer cottages. Much of the rest of the Tjust archipelago is sparsely populated.

STORA ALSKÄR NORTH OF SANDHAMN (pp. 52–53). An evening lull in the outer reaches of the Stockholm archipelago. The smooth, bedrock gneiss is typical: this island once lay under a three kilometre-thick covering of ice, and is still recovering: land in this area rises about 40 centimetres a year — in the Viking days, the island was scarcely a reef beneath the water surface.

DUVHOLMEN OUTSIDE LIDINGÖ ISLAND (pp. 54–55). Morning light over the Höggarnsfjärden Passage. In Stockholm, the idyllic archipelago is never far off; this islet, ten short kilometres from downtown, is where channels to the different city harbours diverge. Much of Stockholm is in fact built on the archipelago's inner islands.

NORRPADA ISLANDS (p. 56). The extensive mass of islands from Landsort in the south to Arholma in the north is generally defined as the Stockholm archipelago. It encompasses 24,000 islands, and at its widest part, directly opposite Stockholm, the archipelago stretches 80 kilometres from the mainland to the outermost skerries at Svenska Högarna. The islands have no troublesome tidal changes; it is easy to make land and easy to find your own quiet, private anchorages.

THE GREEN HILLS OF HÄGGVIK (pp. 58—59). From a lookout on Stortorget Hill in Nordingrå, there is a sumptuous view of Häggvik village, Gaviksfjärden Bay and the rugged coast of the Gulf of Bothnia. This is a coastline of panoramas, living up to its Swedish name: Höga Kusten, or High Coast. The name is actually a recent, tourism-driven invention, but this is undeniably the highest, steepest stretch of coast in the entire Baltic Sea, with mountains of almost 300 metres above sea level.

VIEW OF VÅGSFJÄRDEN BAY (p. 60). The entire coastline from the mouth of the Ångermanälven River to Skag Point has recently been added to the United Nations World Heritage List — for its steep and wild mountains but principally for the swift land elevation: the rock is rising from the sea at a rate of almost a centimetre per year.

NORRFÄLLSVIKEN BAY (pp. 62—63). Furthest out on a point in Ulösundet Bay is Norrfällsviken, a genuine fishing village and one of Ångermanland province's popular holiday resorts. Along the water, old boathouses fight for elbow-room with a restaurant and a fish shop, while up on the hillside there are chalets and a golf course.

HÖGBONDEN LIGHTHOUSE IN ÅNGERMANLAND (p. 64). Atop the bent, granite back of Högbonden, 60 metres above sea level, is a lighthouse built and manned in 1909. At most, 21 people lived here, with a school in the attic. In 1963, the lighthouse was automated and has subsequently been rebuilt as a hostel. The land around is rugged and hilly, notorious for its variable weather. The harbour is unprotected and on windy days, it can be impossible to make land.

FARMLAND

In mid-April, marsh harriers fly in over the wet meadows of Angarn, the wagtails have arrived, hedge sparrows are chirping in the spruces, the meadow pipit bounces out from between tussocks and the osprey sails over the ancient Långhundraled trail.

Soon, the sun is x-raying the newly opened leaves. The sky lightens, and stars fade like dying distress rockets. Birch leaves sprinkle their green dew over branches. White wood anemones lower their petals on to the pungent remains of last year's leaves. Wild chervil wanders, against the breeze, across fields. The pied fly-catcher has arrived via air-mail from Gibraltar. Previously, I was gazing upon Skåne, Sweden's southern-most province, embedded in fog, the tops of the beech trees along Söderås Ridge candied with frost, when a light breeze ploughed a channel through the fog bank. Whitened farms glisten tiredly, as the first lapwings hop on to tufts in the stubbled field, searching for snow-free grazing. An Easter storm lets loose. Dry branches rattle like eggshells. There is a blue anemone light between black tree trunks.

At April's end, brimstone butterflies awaken in the blueberry thickets. Peacock butterflies mate. Aloft, the lark ascends his tonal ladder, is tossed by an invisible hand and rests awhile on a stone by a ditch bank. It heralds a season of courage and light; no lark, no summer — may the thrush and the nightingale sing their hearts out.

The southern region of Österlen, famed for its summer population of artists and writers, is most beautiful in May when its clouds of apple blossoms follow the fishing villages along the coast and broom blossoms like fire in the sand. Around Stenshuvud, Vitaby and Ravlunda there is ancient calm, both Nordic and classic, and sea and bauta stone. Clay-dust spews from a harrowing tractor. The farmer is in haste, while city-dwellers relax in contemplative peace, sheltered from the wind by cliffs which once protected a Viking family. The hats of bitter acorns are spread about as though recently spat out by our forefathers. The scenery was beautiful even in those times, but was never an idyll there was time to enjoy. Endurance, thrift and adjustment to the light were the conditions of survival in Sweden for both nature and people.

One May evening, a hobby falcon is chasing cockchafers and dragonflies and the low, white farmhouses are fluorescent, disseminating that homely feeling you associate with the flatlands of Skåne province. The snipe plays its fret-saw. A buzzard hangs poised in the air, as brown as moist pine needles, over chickens and ducklings. A moorhen or water rail hides in last year's yellow-gold reeds, where the mud keeps all animals of prey, including man, at bay. Spring arrives with the robin and the wild honeysuckle whose scent fills the few hours of darkness when larks are silent. A wagtail prances on the roof ridge. Starlings glitter: a burst necklace, its stones sprayed in all directions. They turn in the air, their calls shining. The May rain forces up marsh marigold, lilies-of-the-valley, cowslips. Black-backed gulls gulp down bleak and Baltic herring, heads first. Everything is movement.

Spring Sundays are for gathering morels, putting birch twigs in vases to bud, turning the compost, fertilising the hotbeds, listening to cuckoos and watching the petals of the wood anemone respond to the passage of the sun. The first crocuses are pilot flames deep in the grass. Soon there'll be a haze of pasque-flowers, dusky purple, furry and ball-like, to mix with the meadow saxifrage bending in the wind. The freshly ploughed fields shimmer like coal. The spring night keeps the mornings and evenings in balance; the oaks stand black, mist blurring the borders of the day. It is easy to see how paths were beaten by cattle, traders, bandits; they broadened into roads, were paved with stone, kept open, grew and were tarred with asphalt, to become highways enclosed by fences against game. Once more, we must choose the narrow gravel or clay roads if we are to see the country as it once was — and, in large part, still is.

One's homeland is ground that flourishes, tilled fields, streets we have walked. Whether or not we have left it all behind, origins remain: roots, a returning, rivers flowing to the sea, sea that ensnares islands and points, hills that shade forest and plain, the garden smell of apple and peony, bunches of rowanberries in a bicycle basket, a lawnmower that chokes and seizes, that jug of buttercups and bluebells on the kitchen table.

Two forces have set their stamp on the Swedish landscape: the ice ages and man. A three kilometre-high glacier depressed the Stockholm area a hundred and fifty metres. At the beginning of the 21st century BC, the land was twenty-five metres higher, and fragments of Stone Age pottery dating from that time have been found to the south-west of the city. The land around Stockholm rose about forty-five centimetres per century. The gift of the ice ages — not only to the hydropower companies — is the varied coastline, the rivers and the streams.

Sweden rests on firm ground. Wind, water and the ice ages have scraped forth the Archaen rock in its hardest and purest form, foreign to alps and vertical limestone strata. The inland glaciers gave us almost a hundred thousand lakes. The pre-glacial ones are deep and have no islands: poor, acidic woodland meres, sandy-bottomed lakes with little nutrient and, most commonly, forest lakes among moraine and rock out-crops, thin reeds and light brown water. Cultivated land is the work of man and grazing animals. Nature has had to make way for these intrusions. Take common tansy (*Tanacetum vulgare*), often seen on the banks of roadside ditches, once a preferred medicinal herb and flavouring for aquavit. In its wild state, it grows only on sea coasts and the remote reaches of archipelagoes; inland, it has spread through cultivation.

Everywhere there are cut-off points in time, meetings between now and the past. Ancient castles, dolmens and stone circles are sometimes as densely prevalent as weekend cottages. Between them, there once were roadways; close to them, there were dwellings where women baked bread of barley and oats, the Iron Age mixture.

Dislocations in nature, drying-out and draining, the elevation of the land and diverted water courses changed people's lives. What was once central became peripheral. Birka, Sigtuna, Gamla Uppsala, Kungälv, Skanör — now mostly memories — were once vital crossroads for trade and shipping. Carl Linnaeus comforts us with his assurance that despite all, our climate is the best: few ever froze to death, fields were not burnt dry but were protected by the snow he called "purest diamond powder". Those in southern climes have spoiled water and muddy roads; we travel on crystal ice over lakes and marshes. Our winter nights are lit by snow and the Northern Lights; we have no deadly animals and more edible wild fowl than anywhere. And in winter, when ice and frost bind lakes and fens, we travel over landscape as straight as the crow flies.

Sweden's landscape is its seasons. The land changes guise from winter to summer. In the summer break, Swedes return to their origins and bond with each other over wild strawberries, freshwater crayfish, Baltic herring, pickled herring and ice-cold aquavit. There is the realisation that even our cities with their parks and treed avenues are part of a cultivated landscape. Summer is our spiritual winter fodder, wrote Harry Martinson, a great Swedish nature lyricist.

The forest meadow, that "Arcadian shepherd's meadow, the hay-field of ancient Swedish farmland, is among the most beautiful, singular and ingenious of all that man was able to create while we still tended the earth on its own terms, as it should be tended if life is to go forward." (Peter Nilson) The landscape that appeals to most of the world's people — according to an American folklore researcher cited by Nilson is the ancient Swedish meadow: stretches of grass interspersed with shady trees and leafy copses. Paths trodden in the grass as though others' steps had recently preceded ours. We want to recognise, rather than pioneer. Art, too, indicates that this is our image of the Garden. There, the groves thinned by man and grazed by animals are free; there, childhood whispers in the birch branches hard by the farmhouse.

The history of people, countryside, cattle and grains is common and interwoven. The forest meadow of the Iron Age and the era of the Great Migration is the cradle of the inhabitants of the Nordic region; it has witnessed work, dreams and crushed hopes, and a circle of life only now being broken. Meadow, pasture, paddock, ploughed field and sowed, succeeded the deep forests which Stone Age hunters were to burn-beat, clear and where they would put down their own roots. Beyond fields, river slopes, rock outcrops and meadows is the hint of a harsher, more antagonistic landscape.

Small-scale forests were important for farm households. Leaves were winter fodder for domestic animals, before the time of sycthes. Lime-trees and ashes with their tops lopped off on southern Swedish farms bear witness to a time when leaves were made use of, through drying and chopping: ash leaves for horses, lime leaves for cows.

Delicate wild herbs have been forced to cede to flora more suitable for grazers, such as yarrow, prunella, white clover, buttonweed and silverweed, most of them migrants from coastal fields. Parklands and coastal landscapes merge — the noble and the savage meet — not least in Södermanland, the province of country estates. When pear trees are left to go wild, they develop thorns; hawthorn, wild rose and sloe are some of the thorn bushes of the pasture.

To live, a landscape must echo others. No intrusion should be more severe than it may allow the land to be restored, should future generations wish it. Today, farms are being closed down, spruce planted in straight rows, and sallow and juniper and aspen brushwood invade. The old peasant-culture landscape, shaped by poly-enterprise, is giving way to a more industrialised landscape of few traditions and more rationalised agriculture and silviculture. The open landscape is shrinking. Ancient history is under threat. The growing of things is not good *per se*. Hornborgasjön Lake, famed for its migratory storks, was once drained to reclaim farmland, though it was once the hub of a striking countryside. It had fish and fertile banks. Suburbs, farms, landing places are situated on arable soil; previously, dwellings were placed on hills to avoid using precious dirt.

The bogs of Öland island have been drained, its bare limestone soil thinned out, its topsoil ravaged by an irate easterly wind and a stubborn westerly. What was once the rich backbone of the island is now a worn steppe, splendid in its barrenness. Grazing has caused further erosion. In the early 19th century, when the central plain ceased to be crown property and was divided among village communities, individual landowners were given titles and built stone walls between the properties.

The floral display of the meadows is richer than that of the pastures where the flora are made invisible by grazing. But where the cattle cease grazing, the wild takes over again — as on the heather moors of Halland province or the meadowlands of Småland. No landscape retains a fixed set design. Conservation measures have been adopted and there is an awakening. National interest and the chance to be included on the World Heritage list have fuelled a renaissance for conservation.

Nature reserves — of which Sweden has far more than most people realise — teach us how nature should be treated to be of use to people, animals and flora. Lake Tåkern in Västergötland province is a good example of an environment that has been saved; there, a reed warblers' chorus floats up from tranquil reed cathedrals. These days, there is no construction without consideration for archaeology, history, water and the topographical profile. The cultivated landscape demands continuous, gentle care to subsist.

Cultivated landscape is neither wasteland nor wilderness; it speaks to us with a human voice, since human generations and recognisable traditions have shaped its parklands, pastures and fields. The swift stenography of arctic terns in the sky fills us with the same peace as treetops and the buzzing of bees and bumblebees. We rest in nature without having to decipher its relentless script. The real absence of ego is elsewhere, in the rainforest and the polar wastes.

The more accessible the wilderness becomes — mountaintops, the outer archipelago islands, the northern moors — the more often people seek it out to wash off city stress. But our feeling for nature is basically characterised by the Arcadian dream, by the cross between forest and cultivated landscape, by gooseberry bushes and forest meadows, perch fishing grounds and wild strawberry slopes. There is a wind over the beet fields, echoing as with Bronze Age horns when it sweeps through burial mounds, meadows that have been erased and ancient forest that has been burn-beaten. What was once forest and lake has become undulating plain, and in the old wetlands, black clay still demarcates the boundary between land and water.

For us Swedes, Carl Linnaeus is not principally the cataloguer who listed and labelled every living thing; rather, the one who taught us to travel and to take nothing for granted, the one who found in nature both fellowship and a way of relating to Creation. Linnaeus joins with everyone who, through the centuries, "loves study, understands the same, favours it and with common sense excels in it".

Linnaeus's journeys of discovery took him through an unknown and unreported country. When riding across the southern plain in 1749, he noted how "villages smelled from a distance of hemp, peat smoke and elderberry blossom". What he observed on the islands of Öland and Gotland is as remarkable as that which his pupils discovered in the tropics. In his day, the province of Dalarna swarmed with beaver; there were flocks of stags and boar on Öland and no one could dream that there would ever be a dearth of wood grouse and black grouse in Sweden's forests.

Linnaeus enjoins us to hunt, collect beneficial herbs and dig deeper into troves of useful minerals. He is a second Adam, in a newly discovered Eden he does not need to leave. Invisible for so long, it reveals itself to his eyes and he gives names to all its beauty and riches. His thirst for knowledge will not subside. He counsels farmers to plant deciduous trees, "since a farm without trees is like a bald head with no peruke". His works are hymns of praise to the earth and to mankind's management of divine materials, even if Nemesis broods in the background.

Kinnekulle could well be an emblem of Sweden's cultivated landscape: its hanging gardens or series of terraces, with coiling roads above the plain, ivy wrapped around old tree trunks, Lake Vänern with its forested, rocky islets, manor estates with beeches and walnut trees. There are tumbling brooks, deepening caves, opening glens and clearings. Church steeples are thicker on the ground here than anywhere, with most from the first centuries of Christianity's advent in this country. The graves are aged:

stone coffins with clumsy lettering from the days of Catholicism.

Linnaeus wrote of the groves on Kinnekulle's northern slopes: "gardens rather than parks, making this place more pleasant than any in Sweden, such that the summer splendour of the manor estates at Hönssäter, Hellekis and Råbäck, situated on the Vänern lakeside, can scarcely be adequately described". Words are seldom sufficient. We Swedes have a taciturnity vis-à-vis nature, as when author Carl Jonas Love Almqvist, in his *Svenska fattigdomens betydelse* (The Meaning of Swedish Poverty) succumbs to the spectacle of the Uppland region where he was raised: "Here, nature is a quiet, introverted schoolgirl, very cautious, not entering the parlour, there to be treated rudely. She whispers slow and talks soft, or rather not soft but as the Aeolian harp from a wonderful distance: the finest ear is needed, the most delicate, most skittish feeling to perceive such beauties as might be destined to eternal concealment."

At that time — the 19th century — horseradish and rhubarb were as widespread as nettles. What appeared to be weeds was good enough to eat. Comfrey and lungwort had blessed qualities now being rediscovered in this age of natural medicines. The fatigue that can visit us in spring used to be a symptom of post-winter scurvy; nettle soup was the prescription until southern fruits became affordable.

Up until the 1920s, small Swedish towns were not divorced from the landscape; their streets were like highways, low wooden houses with green garden patches clustered close to church and courthouse, and cattle roaming through the town if it were too small for city gates and toll house.

In our day, herb gardens are being cultivated again: bloodroot and soapwort, the verbena's pale pink flowers on its rough stalks, Moses's burning bush, thorn apple that produces truth serum — and sage, mint, thyme, chervil … Sten Selander, the early 20th-century author and botanist, sets the scene:

"The scent of catmint and motherwort hit us as from a world of the past: a world of sun-baked wooden fences, behind which a dinner table has been laid between lavender rows, with the paterfamilias reading at the table, while apple blossom snowed down upon the ham and the tankard of weak beer; of white roads, where time drove at a leisure-ly pace in a surrey or a stagecoach; of vicarage gardens, where the disquisitive and the learned Doctor of economics and botany hastened to greet the scholar Linnaeus as he dismounted his horse to rest a while during his journey through Flora's green domain."

I recall a guesthouse in Södermanland province. A melon showed its bald pate over the edge of the hotbed. Around the back, nettles tall as a man hid the compost heap. A white shell here and there indicated where once had been gravel paths. The guests gathered lupin seeds in matchboxes, to rattle a promise of yet another summer. White garden furniture was falling apart in the shimmering air, destined for October's leaf bonfires. The fare was pike-perch from Lake Mälardalen, roast joint and blueberry pie. The shelves held volumes gleaned from some municipal library. The guesthouse was to become an institution, to which travellers adapted. Other guesthouses developed into conference hotels. Chalets, trailer caravans and marquees ultimately replaced a lifestyle that once was common and appreciated. A few remain, however.

Today in Sweden, we can see among grave mounds and relics where alders and willows and reeds register furrows where once rivers ran, and sallow bush and juniper conceal abandoned fields. A grey barn is as transparent as fishbone, and the path towards the wood is barred by fallen trunks. Sour apple trees, wild pears and gooseberries are monuments to a croft as forgotten as junk mail in a summer tenant's letterbox.

In the old days, children were more common than furniture in country cottages, and those who were neither day-workers nor tenant farmers made their living tending many kinds of animals, in contrast to today's specialisation into chicken, turkey, mink or ostrich ... Despite self-subsistent house-holding based on fishing, hunting, chickens and domestic pigs general stores were far more common. Smells emanated from store-houses, earth cellars, from barns and general stores in the old days. Perhaps even the seasons had different smells: more sweat, apples in the attic, privies and wet fertiliser. Outdoor smells came from linseed-oiled timber, chopping blocks and wood shavings. At that time, the forest was still a larder and a blessed apothecary.

Stone walls in the province of Småland and on the islands of Gotland and Öland — around pasture-land, birch copses and fields, belong to the countless number of lines on our earth which serve to delineate territory, cultivation, property. Mossy fields recall former ice-locked lakes. Ancient names echo from the wells of time to tell of the bondsmen, soldiers and serfs who dragged stones to the field cairns and broke the ground before tractors came. For centuries there was a ban on felling oaks, even if they were in the middle of a field; they were the property of the Crown and were to be used primarily for ship-building. This privilege was not abandoned until the 19th century, at which point farm oaks were widely cut down.

On Gotland in May, people gather on the commons. They glean and collect twigs and branches — and have a party. It is one of the great days of summer. Junipers are left for timber and tool-making. Later, the fields will blossom with cowslip and early purple orchids and white butterfly orchis, until the July hay-making. In autumn, the hazels are thinned out and branches lopped off lime and ash and oak. The hay in the fields smells of flowers and fertilises the fields. This field-work is valuable husbandry: the opposite of clear-cutting.

Sten Selander has depicted the southern Swedish landscape of the Stone Age hunters: an ancient forest of deciduous trees unbroken except by the pines of the gravel ridges, the saw grassed bogs and the lakes with their alder marshes and willow thickets. European bison, boar and urus trampled through the marshy forests, with black storks sailing over the treetops. Hardwood trees reached the southernmost Swedish province of Skåne by 6500 BC when ice still covered the country's northern inland. From 3000 BC, the inhabitants had sheep, goats and pigs. Their first crops were beans and barley. In the Bronze Age, horses were tamed and settlement produced population growth.

The transition from the 19th century to the new machinery of the mid-20th century changed Sweden's agricultural landscape. The change dismantled communities and each farmer became a small businessman on his own. A spirit of community, a cultural tradition and a mutual responsibility were broken. The shared grazing pastures and co-ownerships were largely done away with, the commons distributed among plot owners, planted with spruce and pine or turned to the plough.

Villages made up of densely packed houses are rare in Sweden, if you leave aside fishing villages. The village of Stensjö, north of Oskarshamn in southern Sweden has been preserved, with its hop-poles, beehives, cherry orchards, cabbage and spice gardens, smithy and flax retting. And roads became straighter with each generation. Cars do not like sharp corners. The old village roads avoided each obstacle, slinking around oaks, boulders and the farmstead well, taking time to wait for oncoming traffic.

Rocky outcrops were blasted to make the roads straighter, a pine-covered ridge would be shovelled away to a quarry, a wet meadow would become a field of oats, a reedy lake a golf course. Change is natural. But gazebos can be put to new use, as can a hen house and a smithy. Rarer are the old outhouses where wasps gnawed and death-watch beetles clucked: they are wall-papered with old newspapers and print reproductions of the Royal Family, blotched with damp, with an immovable spiderweb and a tiny, fly-spotted window, a hand basin on an iron support, a bowl of grass that one threw over the privy hole to smother the odour. Everywhere there are traces of the structural reforms made in the 1950s and '60s: abandoned railways, brick works and dairies, flooded mine shafts, farming fields turned into forest plantations from Småland in the south to Lappland in the north.

Now, energy pylons stretch nets across the land. Combine harvesters, new in the 1960s, delivered the grain directly to silos. The countryside was depleted of people, mills were closed and people gravitated to urban production and service.

The wooden boxes of the Filadelfia evangelical church, the Ebenezer church's chapels, all gingerbread carpentry, and the IOGT temperance group's union house have all been sold to summer residents with or without the faith. Even petrol stations are acquiring heritage certification; the general store's manual petrol pumps that the freeways made obsolete now seem as ancient as Viking graves. At the same time, mechanisation and automation are giving birth to a new feeling for origins. Local folklore is enjoying a renaissance. "Dig at your feet" is a fond motto for the age of cheap charter travel. IT developments allow many more to live in the country and take care of their businesses remotely. On Gotland, I know several people whose jobs are in New York and Munich and who depend successfully on electronics for the connection.

The old village with its conformism and stifled feeling is history, but in many places, the countryside is in the process of being rediscovered. The residue of agricultural landscape is recycled and put into new pictures in different frames. Partitioned and vanished villages resurface as hordes of amateur genealogists seek out their roots. Increasingly many are looking back to understand themselves and discern a future. Today, most Swedes live in cities, but they still come from the countryside.

The neglect that was tangible from the Second World War until the end of the 1970s in the spirit of hair-raising amortisation and inadequate upkeep is less common now. Cement sheeting is, in my eyes, the ugliest of all house coverings, but the old red copper ruddle has come back since plastic paints were found to cause suffocation and mould, and the reed matting that pushed up like islands through the plastering has been plastered over. Run-down houses resembling manors and dilapidated mansions on the outskirts of towns are being repainted and given new foundations.

There are new meeting places: chalet villages, camping sites, running tracks, canoeing waters, ski trails and hiking routes. A string of eco-museums covers part of the land-scape and we travel between old cattle sheds and smithies, museums and charcoal stacks, sawmills and iron mills, abandoned mines and modern wind-power plants.

As cranes trumpet under the greyest of skies, I visualise a ragged soldier from the 17th century army of Karl XII, trudging homeward across Siberia after release from captivity, bog water in his flask, and obsessively wishing that his wife be dead rather than be out in the harvest field with another man.

In April, winds begin to shake up the ice in the lake-bowls. The edges loosen first. Finally, the sun sucks up the ice over the coldest deep. Grey floes are left along the banks, moiling and rotting like fish meat. A half-moon shines through the cat's cradle of last year's twigs in a magpie nest. The nest has been constructed without a single nail — as barns used to be — and yet will weather a force-ten gale.

Blyth's reed warbler, actually a Russian native, has invaded central Sweden's reedy lakes; many rate its song as best of all. But at night, late in June, it is more common to hear the sedge-warbler from the darkness of the reeds; he has been called the voice of the Swedish summer night. Grebes rasp, coots click, ducks bleat and water rails hammer to show the sun they are still awake. Once in a rare while, by Lake Tåkern or some inlet in Lake Mälaren, the bittern beats and bellows behind the yellow and purple loosestrife on the bank.

When you have accomplished something as Swedish as gathering wild herbs and spices to flavour the winter's aquavit, you sense the magic in re-creating scenes of summer: wet meadows where wormwood stands like dusty silver with the bitterness of centuries in its leaves, the pond with its bog-myrtle, the moor with its juniper. Endless mornings, anticipatory as a sailboat with yet-lashed sail, but no less miracu-lous because you have experienced them an entire lifetime. The dawn blows bubbles in the thin glass of the lakes. Mint is crushed between fingers: discovery and return have equal weight.

Mosquitoes cluster like dandelion fluff around the junipers and the dandelions' own seed globes are lampshades of the latest style, with a white glowing button at the centre. Yellow rudbeckia sways by the cottage corner. The high summer landscape is bulging and plump, like a tapestry stretched by wind. Swedish whitebeam are subdued white by an abandoned dwelling with a crumbling stone foundation. But you can

75

hear the voices of the crofters under trees which once gave fruit for chicken feed and pancake batter. In heaven, says one of them, there are no mosquitoes.

The pasture is veiled in bent grass and tufted-hair grass, their bushy panicles spreading a magic mist over fields and hills. German catchflies glow and daisies gather in phalanxes. Rock-roses are ground-level miniatures. Harebells and bird's-foot trefoils spread themselves out like a wind-torn Swedish flag.

July is less reliable than August, but finally there is one of those hot, summer evenings when the sky slowly empties of light and birds glide silently between the trees before they find their night's rest — an evening when you tread softly, not to disturb the smells and colours. And above the August sky stretches the vault of the Milky Way, like the breastbone of a Greenland whale.

The tawny owl's baleful cry is heard on September evenings. "Between owl wings burn/the galaxy serpent's shiny scales", wrote the Swedish Nobel Prize winner Erik Axel Karlfeldt. The swallows have moved off but the sea is still luke-warm. Two flies meet in a last sparkle. The acorns darken. The day is bluebell-clear.

Cabbage leaves gleam slate-blue in the vegetable bed. In the flowerbeds, asters and marigolds are on fire. The tracks of birds have patterned the garden furniture. The dill is yellowing, but yarrow and bluebells are blooming again. Clitocybe fungi are white against the grass. A finch bounces between branches like a shuttlecock.

Rose hip signals red but the waxwings attack them anyway. A magpie's wing shines like a rear-view mirror above them. The stars are grouping their forces.

In the back-lighting of October, spider-webs appear as thin as frozen breath. Potato tops blaze. Broken greenhouse panes. Snails cross the road for the last time. The witches' eggs of the stinkhorn stick up through the moist spruce needle carpet. Redpolls jingle in the alder tops. Rowanberries radiate impoverished fun. The grass is rusting but light falls as sharp as a scythe over it. Ice seals the lakes, riverbeds resemble unploughed roads through the silent landscape.

The ice is knife-blade thin on the edge of the lakes. Yellow birch leaves, darkened ash leaves and the red of the maple have floated down and stuck; the thinnest of frost threads anchor them to the ice and stop them blowing away. Eventually they will be encapsulated in darkish glass and skaters will be able to glimpse the autumn colours through winter's blurred lens.

Per Wästberg

76

81 FARMLAND

DRYING-RACKS IN SMÅLAND PROVINCE (p. 77). Long hay racks stand in compact columns in the low sun, framed by the field's dark-leaved trees. Behind the closed gate is the old road. This is roughly how paradise must look: old farmland of field and meadow, a light clearing in the forest with lush growth and harvested winter fodder. The promise of food and safety adds even more beauty. In Swedish, there is a shared word for small meadow and well-being: *lycka*.

FENCED FIELDS IN SMÅLAND PROVINCE (pp. 78—9). Fences used to be the hallmark of farmland — labour-intensive constructions that enclosed fields and meadowland. Stone walls were frequent but mostly there were wooden fences. The poles were of juniper and the horizontal filling of fir. In the 1950s, barbed wire replaced wood, then came electric wire. In Bjälebo and in many other places, the old wooden fences are coming back.

COVERED CULTIVATION IN LÖDDEKÖPINGE (p. 80). One of farming's new methods is cultivation under plastic. Long plastic sheets create enormous hotbeds and keep pests away. This promotes fast growth and earlier harvests, and removes the need for chemical spraying. Here, the plastic hides carrots.

FARMING COUNTRY IN LAPPLAND (p. 81). Hay racks stand in the fields of Örträsk as they have for hundreds of years but in the middle distance, silage bales form neat rows along the village road. Pressure-packed grass, sealed in plastic, releases farmers from their near-total dependence on the weather. But cattle need a little dry hay, and hay racks still have a use.

HIGHWAY JUNCTION ON THE SKÅNE PLAIN (opposite). Today's wide, paved roads cut like scars across the countryside: "whip weals", as author Elin Wägner described them as early as the 1930s. But there is a kind of beauty in these modern road patterns: here, Highway E6 meets the E4 outside of Helsingborg, one of the larger cities on Sweden's southernmost coast. The roads almost form a G clef on the fields — less a weal than a musical note on the landscape!

FIELDS NEAR SKÅRBY (pp. 84–5). Fields roll across the plains of Skåne in wide, tranquil swells. It is autumn and the combine harvesters have begun their work. Straw is next: it will be pressed into rock-hard cylinders which are often left in the stubble long into the autumn.

SPRING PLANTING AND RIPENING OATS (pp. 86–7). Farmers are also landscape artists in a very literal sense. They are constantly giving their surroundings new patterns and colours: they plough the land dark, sow it green, harvest it yellow — the picture changing continually. Sprouting spring plants describe soft, constructivist waves in the Västergötland soil, but swiftly the scene will change to green. And a field of oats lights up the hillocks of Halland, creating a colouristic contrast to the green around.

STONY LANDSCAPE IN SMÅLAND (opposite). Walls and piles of stones in the stoniest of stony realms: Krokshult in the middle of Småland province. These are monuments to hardship and the landscape is redolent of sweat, strain and aching backs. There was more to it than pulling up the stones and stacking them; the worst part was finding soil to fill the holes that were left. Clearing went on for centuries but it is now mostly in vain: there are EU grants available for maintaining stone walls and the small fields they enclose but mostly, these cleared fields are left to become forest.

FIELDS AND MEADOWS AT ÅSENS BY (p. 90). Narrow fields surrounded by stone walls, a new fence, grain drying on stooks and a grazing meadow — this was much how farmland used to look. In places it still does, especially in Småland, where farmers cling stubbornly to old habits and traditions. Some use neither tractor nor combine harvester.

BURNING STRAW IN SKÅNE PROVINCE (p. 91). In the old days, straw was always strewn in stables and barns, returning to the soil with the manure. But grain farmers now seldom keep cattle and prefer to burn the straw in the fields, returning some of the nutrition directly.

THE GREAT LIMESTONE PLAIN ON ÖLAND (pp. 92—3). Yellow stonecrop and purple chives light up the dark earth on Stora Alvaret, the strange limestone plain in the middle of Öland Island. Despite appearances, this landscape has been farmland for millennia. Grazing animals are chiefly responsible for the unusual environment, and if they disappear — and chances are they will — much of the plain will become overgrown with bushes and trees.

VISINGSÖ ISLAND AND LAKE VÄTTERN (opposite). Sweden's second-biggest lake is known for its deep and clear water and feared for its capriciousness: suddenly and unexpectedly, its waters can become rough and dangerous. Visingsö is an old, established centre of culture; it was a royal seat in the 12th and 13th centuries. Näs Fortress, now only a ruin on the southern tip of the island, was probably built by King Sverker the Elder.

HEATHER MOOR IN HALLAND (pp. 96–7). The southern Swedish heather moors are very old cultivated landscapes, the oldest created as early as the Bronze Age. This was grazing country and there used to be mile upon mile of heather moors in Halland and the other southern provinces. Most are gone, overgrown and turned to forest. There are a few protected moors left and a large number of place names incorporating the word for heather, *ljung*.

A CHURCH SETTLEMENT IN SMÅLAND (pp. 98–9). The church at Gärdserum was built in the 1850s, at a time when dark and old church buildings were being torn down to make room for big, white structures. The new buildings were called 'Tegnér boxes' after the bishop of Växjö, who was forcing through the modernisation. The church was embellished with spires and pointed neo-Gothic windows, unusual for the time. Previously, there was a stave church on the site, one of the last in Sweden when it was torn down in 1854. The settlement is now a museum, with church services only every third Sunday and no resident priest. The only activity is in the parish hall, where local meetings are scheduled almost every evening.

HAY RACKS IN JÄMTLAND (opposite). A hay field by Kallsjön Lake. Hay is drying on long racks in the traditional way, and the field barns are well-kept and in use. This is old, northern Swedish farmland as it remains in many places.

BARN WALL AT TYSSLINGE IN THE NÄRKE REGION (p. 102). A deciduous sapling, buffeted by wind, has left scratches in the red, copper-based paint as a way of marking out its turf: this spot is mine!

POTATO HARVEST NEAR ÅRE (p. 103). On a late September day in Jämtland province, two men are cutting potato tops with scythes. Shortly, they will use a small tractor to plough open the rows, then pick the potatoes by hand. The empty hay rack and the white silage bales indicate that this is an area where new methods mix with the old.

OAK MEADOW NEAR KINNEKULLE (pp. 104–5). A large oak rests a long branch on the ground in Västergötland. This is an old, settled area where you still find reminders of what once dominated the southern Swedish landscape: oak forests. No other tree possesses such symbolic power and such magnetism; oaks can live a thousand years and for the Celts, Teutons and others, the oak was a holy tree. In Sweden, however, the oak became hated when a 17th century king decreed that all oaks were Crown property — their timber was needed for naval shipbuilding. Farmers were inventive in finding different ways to destroy them: branches were lopped off to induce rot, fires were lit by the trunks and so on.

THE VILLAGE OF STENSJÖ BY IN SMÅLAND (pp. 106–7). This is how the old farming villages appeared before land distribution in the Middle Ages; there are narrow fields, meadows and hayfields of long standing. Stensjö By is a living museum, where the soil is worked by traditional methods, without modern fertilisers, herbicides or combine harvesters. This is farmland before industrialisation.

CHERRY TREES IN BLOSSOM (opposite). This is ancient farmland in Västergötland. Valle county district is well known for its distinctive undulating terrain and its fertile, lime-rich soil. Man has tilled the soil here since the Stone Age — countless archaeological finds and dolmen graves testify to this. The climate is friendly and mild, as the dazzling cherry blossom indicates.

ROCK-CARVINGS AT TANUM (pp. 110—1). Rock-carvings, done three or four
thousand years ago during the Bronze Age (in the north, a couple of thousand years
earlier), are Sweden's oldest preserved art. The most common motifs are boats and
men with weapons and erect penises. The significance was most probably religious but
we know almost nothing of the spiritual beliefs of that time and can only speculate
on the use of the rock-carvings. Many believe they were talismans for the hunt, harvests,
warfare and so on. This carving is unusually well grouped and elegantly executed; it is
one of the most striking art treasures of the Bronze Age. The Tanum Rock-Carvings in
Bohuslän province are included in the United Nations World Heritage List.

A FORD IN THE TORNE ÄLV RIVER (pp. 112—3). The long jetties are actually
a kind of fishing implement. In the old days, wire cages were strung to the poles to
trap salmon; these days, whitefish is the only fish that is caught. The jetties are erected
every spring at spots where whitefish are known to rest on their way upriver. Long
bag nets are used for the fishing, a method that dates back to the Middle Ages. Here,
at Kukkolaforsen Ford, a normal annual catch of whitefish is 20 tonnes.

COW IN VÄSTERGÖTLAND PROVINCE (opposite). A dairy cow in the forest at
Habo — an extremely rare sight these days. To start with, dairy cows are ever fewer;
in 1930 there were more than two million in Sweden, in 2000 only 428,000. Secondly,
dairy cows no longer graze in the woods, since the poor feed there would drastically
reduce milk production. An average cow gives 8 to 10 tonnes of milk a year, which
demands heavy and plentiful fodder. In 1930, cows gave about two tonnes of milk each,
and forest-grazing was common.

121 FARMLAND

KLÖVSJÖ VILLAGE IN JÄMTLAND (pp. 116—7). Klövsjö has been called Sweden's most beautiful village. It lies between steep hills on a slope leading down to a lake. The area has been settled for centuries and is rich in tradition. Summer hay is dried in the old way on racks and cattle are herded to the woods. There are several old field barns still in use — actually an economic necessity for the smallholders here. The village is otherwise best known as a winter sports resort; the western slopes are filigreed by ski runs and ski lifts.

VIEW FROM MATTMAR VILLAGE IN JÄMTLAND (pp. 118—9). What seems to be a lake between the barns and the snow-covered Oviksfjällen Mountains is in fact mist. Under it, however, runs the Indalsälven River, widening to a real lake, Ockesjön Lake.

MID-WINTER, NORTH AND SOUTH (pp. 120—1). Byske village is in Västerbotten province, up north, and the farm on the Varaslätten Plain is in the middle of Västergötland province, far to the south. But the winter experience can be just as intense at both ends of the country, the trees just as heavy with snow and the light just as rosy and glittering.

GRAVEL ROAD IN APRIL (opposite). Typical late winter weather in southern Sweden with fog and slush. There is a hint of purple among the birch branches: the leaf buds are about to burst.

PATTERNS AT STORA BJURUM (p. 124). An April day on the Västgötaslätten Plain: the snow is melting and ploughed furrows rake the landscape.

124 FARMLAND

The Swedish mountains currently enjoy UN protection. An area in the country's north, slightly larger than Luxembourg, has been put on the World Heritage List. It is called Laponia and is recognised as one of the world's unique places demanding special care and attention. The World Heritage area of Laponia consists of four large national parks — Padjelanta, Sarek, Stora Sjöfallet and Muddus — and a vast marsh, Sjaunja. What is unique and worthy of protection is, in other words, the emptiness — this is one of Europe's last real wildernesses: you can hike for days, for weeks, without hearing either chain-saw or car and without meeting a single person. In the middle of Laponia, by Lake Rissajaure between the Padjelanta and Sarek national parks, is Sweden's most remote spot: the nearest road is forty-five kilometres distant.

That is the great, fragile treasure of the Swedish highlands for our time: the silence, the vastness, the space, the solitude. But such goods are not easily marketable and market forces — to the extent they can bring themselves to act in this barren territory — are pushing in the other direction, towards noise and agglomeration. Highlands tourism is following the Continental pattern with large complexes, chalet villages, hotels, ski lifts, piste machines and after-ski facilities. On top of this comes a Swedish speciality: unrestricted snowmobile transport. In Finland, snowmobiles are restricted to trails and in Norway, they are practically banned, but snowmobiles have become part of the lifestyle of northern Sweden and the emblem of freedom.

The wilderness is under pressure, and of all its frail riches, silence is the most threatened, if you define silence as the absence of engine noise. You cannot escape it even by remote Lake Rissajaure; all of a sudden a helicopter will sweep down over the lake, searching for reindeer herds or bear.

But despair is not necessary. The Swedish mountains are still, comparatively speaking, the most untamed, the quietest and most remote to be found in this part of the world, and thereby a heritage to cherish. And one thing needs to be kept in mind: there is room a-plenty, space and scenery in abundance. A mountain chain pushes through Sweden like a gigantic wedge. At the southern end, in Dalarna province, the wedge's width is 850 kilometres, and at the broadest part, in Laponia, there are 1,000 kilometres from the eastern foothills to the Norwegian border in the west. All in all, counting birch forest and highland coniferous forest, the Swedish highlands make up twenty per cent of the country's surface — an area larger than Austria.

And in all that land, there are hardly any inhabitants. About ten roads criss-cross the area, with people living alongside them, but apart from that, only seasonal workers live in the mountains: the semi-nomadic Samis in their summer huts, chalet keepers, hotel staff, piste maintenance staff and glacier researchers.

On a chilly evening in July, I arrive at Kvikkjokk in the interior of Lappland. It is almost midnight and the sun is breaking out from behind Prinskullen Mount and a little wooden church shines like amber in the low light. Getting out of my car, I hear the roar of Kamajåkkås River behind the Tourist Association buildings.

If you want to experience the Swedish mountains at their wildest and most splendid, Kvikkjokk is the right place to begin. The village has been called the Pearl of Lappland and was once a robust economic centre. There was a silver mine here in the 17th century and a parish priest more recently. Sweden's world famous taxonomist Carl Linnaeus arrived here on his Voyage of Discovery to Lappland in 1732. On 6 July, he made his way up to Vallevare Mount and for the first time in his life, found himself above the tree-line: "When I came on the side of it, I seemed to have voyaged to a new world, and when I came to the top, I knew not if I were in Asia or Africa, for the soil, the setting and all herbal growth were unknown to me. I was in the mountains."

After spending the night at the Tourist Association's mountain cabin, I descend to Kvikkjokk and its jetty. This was where the silver smelting works apparently once was. The foundations are still there but the works building itself is gone, swept away by spring floods. The sky is clear and a nippy wind from the west sweeps away the worst of the mosquitoes. The lush Kvikkjokk delta is one of the best haunts in Lappland for mosquitoes; they are part of the cornucopia of the area. Two watercourses meet here:

126

the Kamajåkkå River, turbulent and muddy, and the Tarraätno, tranquil and clear. Between the waters a delta has formed, widely known for its fertility.

In the background rises Mount Vallevare. You don't have to climb very far to reach the tree line and get in among the snow patches. But down in the delta, at the foot of the mountains, vegetation is lusher than anywhere else in the country. Suddenly, you are in a gaudy jungle of grasses and herbs; in southern exposures here and there, the hiker will almost completely disappear under wolf's-bane, shield fern and moorking. It really is like being in Africa or Asia. The soil and light hot-house the plants — lime-rich soil and the midnight sun. It must also be admitted that some of the mountains have poor soil, with rocks lacking lime. There, plant life is quite different: thin and shy. For example, in Dalarna province; on his trip there, Linnaeus noted with disappointment: "I had hoped to find here far more *plantas alpinas novas et raras* than in the Lappland mountains, since we are so much farther south, but was mournfully deceived, as I found not a tenth part of that in Lappland."

There has recently been torrential rain over Kvikkjokk — the most abundant rain for perhaps centuries, and the entire delta has been drenched as though after a severe spring flood. The water has receded and there is a layer of dust on the slopes, a light-brown sedimentary powder. The old hay-fields, willow-thickets, crane's bills, wolf's-bane, alpine bartsia, globeflowers — everything is powdered by soil and sand, and dust billows up on my legs as I set off.

After three hours of unforced walking through forest, I arrive at Njunjes, the last mountain station. People still live here, at least for half the year, and on a doorstep sits a Lappland spitz of some kind, barking at me. I do not approach; there are restriction lines around the house, of the kind used to stop access to roadworks, and small yellow signs indicate a private area. The residents are showing hikers just where they can and cannot go, demonstrating their aversion and frustration. This is the sad end to their history, the highland farmers' bitter farewell. If one cannot live off farming any longer, one can at least live in peace and quiet.

The first farmer arrived here at the end of the 18th century. His name was Holmbom and for five generations, his family was to rule over a vast, highland domain: 2,500 hectares of forest and hay-field. The land was never redistributed in the land reform movement, and at most, there were six part owners, all descendants of Holmbom.

They tilled the fields together and shared the hay according to work input and need.

The writer Carl Fries happened by in the 1950s and was enchanted: "Njunjes," he wrote, "is a memory in reality. The small farmhouses perched on juicy green embankments under the mountain precipices are a scene from Old Norse days: the open farmyards of the Iron Age peasant, the Lidarende Estate with its ice-grey buildings and rich, grassy tussocks, the pastoral origin which is simultaneously the end of history, a thousand-year cultivators' saga."

The saga of Swedish highland cultivators would, however, last no more than a couple of centuries. In Njunjes, it ended in the 1960s, at about the same time as most highland farmers gave up. The whole heroic achievement of mountain farming, culminating at the beginning of the 20th century with all the crown land grants to crofters, is but a short parenthesis in the history of the mountains.

Almost as short as the story of silver mining.

It began in the 1630s, when Chancellor of the Realm Axel Oxenstierna was the main wielder of power in Sweden. It was a harsh time for the country: the Thirty Years War was still being fought, the mighty warship Vasa had only recently sunk on its maiden voyage, and the Älvsborg Ransom — a million *riksdaler* to the Danes for the return of Älsborg Fortress — had made a deep hole in the crown's coffers. Thus, the hopes of many were raised when the Royal Pearl and Diamond Hunter, Jöns Persson, brought home several heavy stones from the Nasafjäll district which were revealed to contain large amounts of both silver and lead.

Axel Oxenstierna ordered the immediate mining of ore and as early as the end of the 1630s, a mining operation was in full swing. A smelting works was built at Silbojokk, fifty kilometres from the mine. The indigent Samis were of course given the heavy work of transporting the ore there. They delivered a thousand sled-loads a year. At most, a couple of hundred Sami men were on the work-force. Everything was painstakingly noted: in 1640, which was a good year, the smelting works produced 33.9 kilograms of silver. Together with the lead, the value of production was 4,700 *riksdaler*. But costs for the same period amounted to 9,350 *riksdaler*.

The Nasafjäll project never made a profit and in 1659, a troop of Norwegians attacked, demolishing both the smelting works and the mine and chasing the workers off. Nasafjäll was right on the still-undefined border and it was unclear whether the mine was in Norway or Sweden. Only in 1751 was the border finally fixed; basically, it went along the top of the mountains, on what is known as the keel. If the water ran eastward, the land was Swedish, and if it ran to the west, Norwegian.

Just before the attack at Nasafjäll, a Sami called Jon Persson had discovered a silver lode about fifty kilometres north-northwest above Kvikkjokk, and in 1661, a smelting works was built at Kamajåkkå. When Linnaeus arrived in 1732, the works still existed, although in name only; production had ceased thirty years previously. The mineral ore they found was poor and it is said that the smelting works at Kvikkjokk produced no more than a couple of kilos of silver a year. But it says a lot about the attraction of silver and the inordinate expectations of the riches of the mountains that such measly results could still keep about a hundred souls occupied. Most were Samis; just as in Nasafjäll they were given the hard work of quarrying the ore and transporting it down to the smelting works. 'Forced' might be more appropriate; silver mining in the mountains is the darkest chapter in the history of Sweden as a colonial power.

Because I am actually in a colony. I am in the middle of what was originally — and still is — called Sameätnam, the Land of the Samis. Njunjes is Sami for 'mountain spur', and there were Sami camps in autumn and spring long before Holmbom came here to settle. If you follow the valley about five kilometres up, you will find a Sami sacrificial site. There is a magnificent natural archway on the precipice below Runka-tjåkko and a *jåkk* or stream that flings itself off the cliff. I climbed up there once and in the loose rock below the stream I found, remarkably, a reindeer skull. I cannot be sure whether it was the remains of a sacrificial offering or something else. Mining company bailiffs, priests and settlers led the colonisation of Sameätnam, beginning in earnest at the end of the 17th century. At the same time as the silver smelting works was founded, Kvikkjokk's first church was built. A chapel was also built on Mount Alkavare, the most northerly Lutheran church of its time. (A chapel still stands.) Concurrently, the first Swedish settlers arrived, waving royal land grants. In 1673, the young King Karl XI had issued a decree granting "freedom for those who would settle the Lappland terrain" — freedom from paying taxes for fifteen years.

It was a grim period for the Samis and many sayings and legends derive from this time. One of the narratives that survive in written form is about the Kvikkjokk silver. It was dictated by Anta Pirak, a Sami from around Luleå, to Harald Grundström some time in the 1930s:

The old people told us this, although I have forgotten almost everything. In the old days, the Swedes were mining silver ore at Silpatjåkko and, if I remember correctly, at Alkavare. And even though the Samis were unwilling, they were forced to fetch the silver ore from Silpatjåkko and Alkavare to Kvikkjokk. It was there that such ore was smelted and then the silver taken further down-country. But some of the Samis did not obey, although they had been ordered to transport the ore. A judge convicted the Samis who did not obey. The justice place was in the north, a distance from Kvikkjokk, close to and under a pine tree called the Justice Pine. All who had been summoned, gathered there. Those who had not obeyed were punished in the following way: for delinquents such as these, two holes were made in the lake ice. The judge determined the distance between them. The delinquent was tied hard to a rope and was pushed down through one of the holes and up through the other. There would have been other methods of punishment to fit the nature of the crime.

The Justice Pine is certainly historically correct. There were many in the Sami lands. There is no record of rope-hauling under ice in Kvikkjokk but there is a written record of it in Nasafjäll.

I tarry a while at Njunjes. The ice-grey houses are semi-dilapidated, their board roofs sunken and rot attacking the log walls and the floors. Soon, all will subside into the profuse vegetation. The only habitable building has recently been given new board facing and a coat of red paint. It looks more like a standard summer cottage than the Lidarende Estate. In the farmyard is a symbol of the new times: a four-wheeled, off-road scooter, a kind of toy car with fat tyres for loose sand and waterlogged terrain. The mountains are heavily motor-dependent these days. In the summer, four-wheelers and helicopters are ubiquitous; in the winter there are snowmobiles — in enormous and virtually unregulated numbers.

All this has changed mountain ways. People up here are reluctant to move about the countryside unaided by engines. If they want to go fishing in a mountain lake or shoot grouse, they may well rent a helicopter there and back. In winter, the snowmobile is unchallenged. Those of us on foot under the weight of heavy backpacks are from the south or abroad. There are Germans, Dutch, Finns and Britons, in roughly that order numarically. There are hardly any skiers, at least not cross-country style. Even tourists have been motorised and no one ever goes up any mountain without being pulled up. It is common to ride a helicopter to some remote peak to hurtle down 'off-piste'.

I once travelled by snowmobile from Kvikkjokk to the Norwegian border and back, so I know what it's like. It took us all of a couple of hours to get to Vaimok, even after stopping at the deserted Holmbom house at Bäcken. Trekking the same distance would take almost three days. The snowmobile has swiftly shrunken the mountain world and the old milestones have lost their validity; a day's journey can take you two hundred kilometres or more. There is nowhere either remote or inaccessible any longer. If you cannot get there by snowmobile, there is always the helicopter.

There is a blanket ban on off-road driving within the national parks but this does not apply to the reindeer-farming Samis. They are allowed to conduct their business without hindrance. The Samis are, by custom, a natural part of mountain life — an integral part of the wilderness. And it is certainly true that reindeer are important for mountain biodiversity, as are all ruminants. It is a mistake to believe that the wilderness would be wilder or more enriched if all human agriculture were eliminated; it is often the contrary, that some farmed environments, especially those under grazing such as pastures, wet meadows and mountain pasture, are the most rich and varied and worthy of protection. But in recent years, reindeer management has become more extensive and streamlined, purely because of the vehicle factor. The reindeer and their owners are separated by greater distances than ever; they graze in semi-feral herds in forests and highlands without any real supervision. The animals are herded together when calves are to be marked or for slaughter, by using helicopters, four-wheelers or snowmobiles. Reindeer are sometimes even loaded on to truck-trailers for transport to winter pastures. Long reindeer fences are being put up between Sami grazing lands, which conflicts with all mountain custom and ruins the wilderness feeling.

Reindeer farming has become just another industry in the economy, with profitability under pressure and lowered margins. And it has had a marked impact on the biology of the highlands and the variety of the wilderness lands. One way to meet greater demands on profitability is to increase turnover, that is, increase the number of reindeer. It is hard to obtain exact figures, but there are about 250,000 reindeer in the mountains, and in periods such as just after the nuclear disaster at Chernobyl in 1986, for example, there have been as many as 300,000. (Radioactive fall-out affected only parts of Västerbotten and Jämtland provinces but almost all reindeer meat became impossible to sell and many owners chose not to slaughter for several years.)

The consequence has been noticeable over-grazing and researchers report diminishing lichen coverage and growing erosion. This can in turn be the reason for recent problems affecting lemmings and other rodents; as early as the 1980s, there were reports that their natural four-year cycles seemed to have been disturbed, the normally recurring years of large rodent populations seemed to have been skipped. This could, in its own turn, explain the decrease in numbers of rough-legged buzzards, and other ecological anomalies. All this is, however, speculation: everything can just as well — perhaps rather — be explained by the weather. Mild pre-winters with a subsequent coating of ice hit both rodents and reindeer hard.

Another consequence of extensive and growing reindeer farming is an increase in the damage caused by predators and rising hostility to these animals. The Swedish Environmental Protection Agency, which has to deal with both the damage and the animosity, reckons that about 30,000 reindeer are killed yearly, mainly by lynxes and wolverines. The Samis get about $3.5 million in compensation but want three times that figure. The radical solution to the reindeer farmers' problem can be summarised in one word: snowmobiles. When the farmers feel they are not receiving adequate compensation, they often counter by trying to reduce losses in their own way — by killing beasts of prey. And no tool has been more deadly and efficient than the snowmobile. In recent decades, in almost all known cases of illegal culling of wolves, bears, wolverines and lynxes, the shooting has been from the saddles of snowmobiles.

Worst hit has been the wolverine. It is an exclusively mountain-dwelling animal and seems to be entirely dependent on reindeer for food. Even though it has been protected since 1969 — purely because snowmobiles had helped increase kills — wolverine numbers have not stabilised. There are still only between two and three hundred wolverines in Sweden with scarcely a hundred lairs. This is certainly due to illegal hunting from snowmobiles; the wolverine is slow and slightly clumsy, especially on snow, and not difficult to catch on a fast snowmobile.

Up on the peaks of Kuravagge, north of the snow-clad Staika, an icy wind bites from the northwest. Frost has been predicted for the night — sad, since the cloudberries are so plentifully in bloom, as are blueberries. There is little life in the valley. I meet only a single pair of golden plovers and from a high rock, a long-tailed skua fixes me with an untroubled stare. The skua is the mountain pirate, actually a sea-bird that normally pillages the Norwegian coast, robbing other sea-birds of their food. But it nests in the mountains, returning faithfully to the same valley, year after year. If rodents are abundant, a skua pair will lay a single egg, after which it is taking your life into your own hands to stray too close to the nest. The long-tailed skua is uncommonly aggressive and dive-bombs intruders, forcing them to duck in panic. At the moment, though, it is perched quietly, following me with its gaze. This could mean rodents are scarce this year again. When I reach the thousand-metre line and come upon the first little lake, Kurajaure, I find there is still ice on the water. It is crumbling and the edges have broken loose from the shore but it is still ice and the date is 7 July. It is a grim feeling.

But the summer of 1732 was similar. Linnaeus's visit coincided with a period of cool weather, which can be deciphered from the rings of cut trees or in glacier sediment. He was probably a few dozen kilometres north of here, on the mountain above Virihaure, when he wrote that he rested for the night rather than proceed, "not daring, in my fatigued state, to cross the ice". He also recounts how he walked through a chill storm and that he sank through the snow, becoming damp and hurting his thigh.

Indeed, I manage to sink through as well, filling my boots with snow. The path is constantly obliterated by thick drifts undermined by water from thawed snow. There are so many pitfalls I decide to turn back down to the valley. I am actually out looking for birds and flowers and thus an old-fashioned hiker — roughing it does not entice me.

The history of mountain hiking is rather brief. It became popular in the early 19th century when a stream of botanists passed along this very trail, from Kvikkjokk towards Virihaure and Sulitelma, partly because Linnaeus had been here and partly because it is an exhilarating area for botany. The botanists were followed by cartographers, glacier researchers and tourists. Sometimes all in the same person, as with the prominent geographer Axel Hamberg, who hiked in Sarek every summer from 1895 to 1930, making cartographic notations, being the first to ascend a score of mountain peaks, studying the larger glaciers and constructing a weather observatory at Pårtefjället. He also built weather-proof huts that he transported to the area and wrote a classic guidebook to Sarek for the Swedish Tourist Association.

When mountain hiking began, it was much like exploring. People carried various instruments: thermometers, barometers, and apparatuses for photography. They measured, made notes, collected, catalogued and documented in the best Linnaean spirit. Their enthusiasm for empirical observation was strong, especially concerning the weather.

Professor Hamberg sent his students to the observatory in Pårtetjåkkå where they were employed measuring temperature, air pressure and humidity at regular intervals — every third hour or so, around the clock, year in and year out. For decades, they produced an enormous wealth of statistics, to almost no purpose at all. Their notations were archived and remain so; their measurement series were, despite everything, far too short and too detailed to provide any data of interest about climate development. Using tree rings and sediment, we have now been able to follow the mountain climate back 1,500 years. Hamberg's observatory still exists, completely intact. I went up there one summer, perhaps in search of the old pioneering spirit, and there everything was, exactly as it had been left seventy years ago: the weather-proof hut, the furniture, the bed linen, the kitchen equipment — it was as though those living there had gone out on an errand, due back at any moment.

Behind the hut, at the foot of the hill, I saw the huge glacier, almost frightening in appearance. My thoughts went to Manne Hofling, one of Hamberg's students, who got lost in sleet-filled darkness on the evening of 25 September 1917. He disappeared, never to be found, and is presumably somewhere down there in the ice. "A martyr to science", wrote Hamberg in the Tourist Association yearbook for 1918.

The mountains are a wild and perilous world, but their attraction is no longer as powerful. Dreams of untold riches swiftly came to nought. In a property appraisal of a highland homestead at Aktse in 1854, there is a dry recording concerning the mighty peak at Skierfe, now part of the World Heritage List: "Mountain. Unusable. Value: 1 *riksdaler*, 16 *skilling*".

And when the first national parks were founded at the beginning of the 20th century, that very lack of usefulness was a deciding argument. Government conservation experts proposed in a 1907 report that the entire area from Torne Marshlands to Aktse should become one single, giant national park. The area was anyway, they wrote, "of almost negligible economic interest".

The protected area did not turn out to be quite that expansive but in 1909, the Sarek and Stora Sjöfallet parks were established as well as Abisko, Pieljekaise and Sonfjället. In all, 350,000 hectares of wilderness, which thus would be protected and preserved untouched for all time. Although not entirely. The experts had miscalculated one aspect: there was in fact something of considerable economic interest in the parks — hydropower. In the Stora Sjöfallet national park was a chain of falls originating from the source lakes of the Stora Luleälv River; they were described by many as Europe's mightiest falls. This was wilderness at its most untamed.

In 1919, the *Riksdag*, or parliament, voted to build hydro dams along the falls and detach the whole river system from the national park. Lake Akkajaure, in the centre of the park, was incorporated into the hydro scheme, and so it came to pass that in the middle of Laponia, protected by the UN's World Heritage programme, is one of Sweden's biggest hydroelectric reservoirs with a water level that can vary by up to 30 metres. Today, there is virtually nothing more that can be done to extend hydropower, and the old conviction is once again valid: the mountain area is of little economic interest. There is no longer any serious commercial threat to the World Heritage site.

Interest from other quarters has also cooled. Scientific curiosity is not as fervent as it used to be: the maps have all been drawn, the flowers all discovered and the peaks all conquered. Even interest in hiking has waned. It reached an apogee in the 1930s and '40s and saw a strong renaissance in the '70s. But since then the backpackers are fewer and the Tourist Association is scaling down its activities in the mountain areas: in Kvikkjokk, you cannot even buy lunch any longer. Which leads one to wonder about the heirs to Laponia: who will safeguard this World Heritage if no one cares about the wilderness? The mountain Samis have packed their bags and now live year round in villages or built-up areas. Only reindeer traverse the mountains alone, and the question is, for how long? In economic terms, reindeer farming is an industry in crisis: of Sweden's 20,000 Samis, only 2,500 are reindeer farmers and of them, perhaps 800 are able to make a living solely from the reindeer business.

But for a few short July weeks, the Samis' summer camps are populated. This is when reindeer calves are marked. And if you are up in the mountains at that time, you can still discover the breathtaking feeling of being in a new, different world.

In the summer of 1986, a few months after the Chernobyl disaster, I came to

Jokkmokk to interview a Sami, Lars-Åke Spiik. He wasn't at home. It was calf-marking time and he was at the summer camp at Arasluokta, deep in Padjelanta.

You cannot get there by car, so photographer Janne Hellberg and I flew from Kvikkjokk to Lake Virihaure, the most striking lake in Lappland. "The water… was milk green or just like water in a basin that has held milk", wrote Linnaeus rapturously.

We then had to walk ten kilometres over Mount Stuor-Titer to get to the Arasluokta camp. Halfway up, we ran into a rainstorm. It came suddenly, like a river rapid, and whipped us off the slope. We were not properly prepared, and we had to use our two flimsy rain capes to rainproof Janne's cameras. When we got off the mountain, drenched to the skin and with water-filled boots, we stumbled into one of the Swedish Tourist Association's cabins. The storm was clawing at the walls and rain beating the windows and on one of the beds lay a young man, reading. He had an academic look to him, perhaps a geologist, and he looked up as we came in.

"We're full," he said.

We looked at each other and turned back out into the rain. Wading a jokk, or stream, which had begun to look like a minor river, we found our way to the small headland where Lars-Åke Spiik's family had their summer camp. They had a traditional tent-like Lapp cot (still used, although most Samis have now built cottages even up in the mountains). We opened the door flap and stepped in. There was an old couple sitting there, obviously Lars-Åke's parents. Lars-Åke himself was asleep, lying by the cot wall with a couple of dogs too tired to even sniff the air when we entered. They had been marking calves all day.

The old people nodded easily at us, but said nothing. We sat down on the floor, covered in the traditional way with reindeer hides over birch twigs, aromatic and comfortable. We emptied our boots outside, wringing out the socks as well. We removed our soaked coats and hung them on a line just inside the entrance, set out our cameras and lenses, and lay down on the reindeer hide. While we were occupied with our wet things, the woman had begun carving slices from a smoked reindeer shoulder. She had brought out some thin, soft Northern bread and some other items, and the man had put a pot of coffee on the fire. When we had had our coffee, bread and reindeer meat and began to feel properly comfortable, the old Sami asked:

"So. What do you want?"

It really was like coming to a different land.

Tommy Hammarström

REINDEER HERD IN LAPPLAND (p. 137). In September, reindeer are driven down from the mountains to be divided among owners and slaughtered. These reindeer belong to the Sami community of Vilhelmina and have just been released from a corral.

LAKE GÄUTAN IN THE WESTERN MOUNTAINS (pp. 138—9). Alongside the lake runs one of the few major roads to cross the highlands, the E79 between Umeå and Mo in Rana. It is known as 'the Blue Road' since it follows the Umeälven River and all its lakes. This picture was taken from the top of Tärnaby's ski run.

RAPASELET IN SAREK NATIONAL PARK (pp. 140—1). The Rapadalen Valley is the gateway to Sarek, the wildest and most inaccessible part of the Swedish highlands. At the foot of the tall, steep Piellorieppe massif the silt-rich Rapaätno River runs through a tropically green valley until it widens to a stretch of smooth water, leaving shallow, nutrient-rich lakes behind it. You can often see moose grazing at some distance from the banks.

A MARSH IN SOUTHERN LAPPLAND (pp. 142—3). Mountain foothill landscape at Njakafjäll with pine moors and wetlands. In the background, Marsfjället Mountain rises steeply, given its dramatic shape by ancient glaciers. This is the southernmost massif of the Lappland alpine belt. The entire mountain, including a large, forested plateau to the east, is a protected reserve.

NORRA STORFJÄLLET MOUNTAIN IN LAPPLAND (opposite). This area is part of the huge Vindelfjällen nature reserve. It was established in 1982 and will ultimately become a new national park. The reserve stretches from Tärnaby to Ammarnäs, from the forests to the Norwegian border, and is the largest reserve in Sweden: 484,000 hectares.

REINDEER IN SAREK NATIONAL PARK (p. 146). Reindeer farming is now completely motorised. Helicopters are used to herd together the semi-wild animals for marking or slaughter and no reindeer owner can manage without four-wheeler motorbikes and snowmobiles. In the autumn, it is not uncommon for reindeer to be transported to forest grazing by truck. The land they graze on is increasingly likely to be enclosed by high, steel mesh fences.

TWO REINDEER IN SAREK NATIONAL PARK (p. 147). A few reindeer are climbing the slope of Mount Skårki, just north of Rapadalen Valley in Lappland. There are about 300,000 reindeer in Sweden and they are important for the mountain ecology. The highland moors are gigantic pastures for the animals and recent reports indicate some over-grazing. But there have always been reindeer in the mountains and they must be seen as a natural — and vital — part of the wilderness.

MOUNTAINS NEAR KVIKKJOKK (pp. 148—9). Autumn birches and mountains above the tree-line are mirrored in the smooth waters of Lake Saggat. A young Carl Linnaeus, later the world's most famous taxonomist, travelled across this lake in 1732 when, during his journey through Lappland, he reached the mountains for the first time. From Kvikkjokk, he walked through Padjelanta district, across Flatjökeln and down to the Norwegian Sea — then briskly back again. There is now a paved road all the way to Kvikkjokk, where tourists travel every summer to walk in the great man's footsteps.

LAKE GRÖVELSJÖN AND MOUNT SALSFJÄLLET (opposite). The mountains in Dalarna are not part of a unified chain but are scattered like massive islands, soft and round in shape, across the forest landscape. The highest point is at Storvätteshågna with its 1,204 metres, just east of Lake Grövelsjön. The bedrock is only thinly covered by soil and the forests are therefore chiefly pine.

SNOWCLOUDS OVER KÄRKEVAGGE IN LAPPLAND (p. 152). Kärkevagge means 'stone valley'. There are a large number of boulders here and in addition the clearest lake in Sweden, Lake Rissajaure.

A MOUNTAIN BIRCH IN LATE AUTUMN (p. 153). Despite its name, the mountain birch is not a true species, rather a knotted, hardy variety of the common white birch. This tree in Stora Sjöfallet National Park is shaped by years of storm winds.

WINTER AT AKTSE (pp. 154–5). On the Rapaälven River delta, at the gateway to Sarek National Park is an old homestead known as Aktse. It is now a familiar resting-place on the Kungsleden Trail, the long route from Abisko to Hemavan. Farming ceased here in the 1960s but the hay barn is still standing. When the old Aktse homestead was being valued in 1854, the magnificent Skierfe mountain terrain was dismissed as useless and the property given a value of just over one *riksdaler*.

WINTER ON TOP OF ÅRESKUTAN MOUNTAIN (pp. 156–7). The peak cabin is snowed under and the odd snow sculpture behind is in reality a communications mast. This is a classic ski-resort mountain with the oldest and biggest winter sports facilities. Sweden's first mountain railway, 800 metres long, was built here in 1909.

UNNA RÄITAVAGGE IN THE KEBNEKAISE MOUNTAINS (opposite). A lone ski trail leads down to the resting-place at the foot of steep Mount Räitatjåkka. Few venture into this narrow, dramatic valley; snowmobile traffic is banned and cross-country skiing is not so common in these mountains.

VIEW FROM SAREKTJÅKKÅ MOUNTAIN (pp. 160–1). We are atop the highest mountain in Sarek (2,089 metres) and the second-highest in Sweden. Sarektjåkkå was first climbed in 1879 by a cartographer, Gustav Wilhelm Bucht, who believed it to be the country's highest point. But the following summer he discovered Mount Kebnekaise to be almost thirty metres higher. The second person to climb Sarektjåkkå was a young Parisian lawyer, Charles Rabot, who made the ascent in 1881. Two years later, Rabot became the first man to climb Kebnekaise.

CLOUDS OVER THE KEBNEKAISE MOUNTAINS (pp. 162–3). Peaks emerge like islands from a cloudy sea, providing vantage points to see cloud movement and formation. For those interested in such phenomena, the mountains are ideal. In the early 20th century, the geographer and mountain pioneer Axel Hamberg built an observatory on a peak in Sarek purely to document cloud formation.

MOUNT KEBNEKAISE (opposite). View from the northern peak over the southern peak, Sweden's highest point at approximately 2,117 metres above sea level — the height varies since the peak has an ice cap more than 40 metres thick. Climbing Kebnekaise has become a popular tourist outing and the trail is well beaten. In the distance can be seen the peaks of Sarek.

A BULL MOOSE IN SAREK NATIONAL PARK (p. 166). The biggest bull moose are in northern Sweden and here in Rapadalen, luxuriant vegetation has nurtured an especially strong and well-built stock. This bull's horns have seventeen tines, but even larger horns are not uncommon in Sarek. This is not because the moose are allowed to grow older but simply because of their size. The horns are largest when the moose is most virile, at seven years, but later decrease in size.

SUN OVER VINDELFJÄLLEN (p. 167). Light plays on Ammarfjällen Mountain and the upper reaches of the Vindelälven River by a smooth water called Framakselet. The Vindelälven is one of the four great protected rivers still undammed.

167 MOUNTAINS

THE REFLECTION OF PIELLORIEPPE MOUNTAIN (pp. 168–9). Sheltered between steep mountainsides is the lush Rapadalen Valley. Moose, bear, wolverine and lynx thrive here and there is abundant bird life with whooper swans, golden eagles, gerfalcons and all kinds of wading birds. This has been called Sweden's Serengeti, a paradise for wildlife unequalled elsewhere in the country.

HIGHLAND DIVERSITY (pp. 170–1). In the highlands, all the mountains, lakes, marshes, rivers, valleys, every little outcrop have been given names by the Samis. These names have now been officially adopted. Following a decision by the National Land Survey, in accordance with UN Resolution No. 36 regarding place names in minority languages, all names used by Samis are to be entered into official maps. This has meant that many places now have two names, such as Kiruna/Giron, Sweden's northernmost city, and Kebnekaise, which can also be written Giebnegáisi.

THE LAISÄLVEN RIVER CANYON (p. 172). The Laisälven flows in the Arjeplogsfjällen Mountains alongside the old Nasa silver mine near the Norwegian border. At Laisstugan, beside the old silver trail, the river cuts a deep cleft in the rock before it reaches wetland and forest.

A WATER STAIRWAY AT SAXNÄS (p. 173). Water rushes wild and unchecked from southern Lappland's Lake Kultsjön down broad rock steps. This is an exciting place for both salmon and salmon anglers. Fishing with hand gear is now free in the mountains, except in national parks or reserves, but you need a fishing permit and must undertake not to disturb reindeer farming or the Samis.

THE ROAD TO VIETAS IN LAPPLAND (opposite). The mail bus heads towards the steep Mount Lulep Kierkau and the glittering water of Langas, a long lake which is actually part of the Stora Luleälven River. We are in the Stora Sjöfallet National Park, but the lake system, including a famous falls, has been tamed for hydropower and detached from park supervision. Thus Stora Sjöfallet is in effect two parks separated by a reservoir at Lake Akkajaure, where the water level can be raised or lowered 30 metres.

THE CHURCH VILLAGE OF KALL IN JÄMTLAND (pp 176—7). In the foothills of Åreskutan Mountain. These days, almost no-one lives in the mountains year-round; the Samis live in urban areas and spend time in the mountains only during the height of the summer. But down in the foothill valleys there are still settlements, albeit small. Here by Kallsjön Lake, farmland is still open and still being worked, although tourism is the most important source of income.

PÅRTEJEKNA GLACIER IN SAREK (opposite). Sweden has more than 300 glaciers with a total area of 300 square kilometres. Pårtejekna is one of the biggest at 11 square kilometres. Contrary to belief, glaciers are not relics of the Ice Age; most were formed about 2,500 years ago when the climate suddenly became colder after the warmth of the Bronze Age. Since then, they have grown or shrunk with changes in the weather.

SUNRISE AT LAPPORTEN (pp. 180—1). View towards the south-east. To the left, Torneträsk Marsh and to the right, Mount Njulla. Between them run a road and a railway: the relatively new E10 highway from Luleå to the Norwegian port of Narvik, and the old iron ore railway completed in 1903.

TARFALADALEN VALLEY AT KEBNEKAISE (pp. 182—3). Glacier research, or glaciology, is an advanced science in Sweden, mainly because of work done here at Tarfala. For more than half a century, researchers have studied the Great Glacier of the Kebnekaise massif, compiling the world's longest series of measurements of glacier mass. Tarfala is a very windy spot and has notched up Sweden's wind-speed record: 81 metres per second.

NORTHERN LIGHTS OVER ABISKO (p. 184). In the old days, people believed the skies were mirroring schools of herring or that swans were frozen and unable to move or that glaciers had absorbed enough energy to become fluorescent. We now know that charged particles colliding with atmospheric molecules produce the phenomenon and that it is visible principally in the Polar regions because of the disposition of the earth's magnetic field. Whether or not the aurora borealis crackles or howls is an open question. Many have heard the lights but no one has yet recorded the sound.

Sweden is a forest realm. From the air, this is very obvious: glinting lakes are surrounded by huge, dark forests, stretching into apparent infinity. More than half the country is covered by forest and an eighth is lake-water — the rest is highland and marsh, with a smidgen of cultivated fields and buildings.

This is Sweden, a land of dark coniferous forest with a few white birch exclamation marks — and frequently, shimmering water. A beautiful country, certainly. And rich: forestry is the nation's only industry that returns a proper surplus.

Coniferous forest dominates almost the entire country, from Tornedalen in the far north down to Skåne, across the Sound from Denmark. This is the northern taiga, extending its lengthy arm across the Scandinavian peninsula — from the forestry point of view, Sweden is actually a part of Siberia. In Sweden's south, however, it is a different story. There flourish the beech, elm, oak and shady leaves. The southernmost provinces should be seen as part of the Continent: Skåne and Halland are, though historically annexed by Sweden these past 250 years, topograpfically still part of Denmark.

There is a region in Sweden where the Continent and Siberia meet, where the tree species are mixed and variety is greater than anywhere else. It is from the southernmost limit of coniferous growth to the northernmost of the oak, from Skåne to the Dalälven River in south-central Sweden, somewhat north of Stockholm. Here, you find majestic, wide belts of coniferous trees but also dark forests of beech and sweeping hillsides of oak trees, old deciduous copses of aspen, ash and elm. This mixed forest roughly covers the ancient kingdoms of the Goths and the Sveas, the original Sweden, and perhaps this is principally the kind of landscape the thoughts of Swedes conjure up when we speak of the forest. Sweden is therefore a forest realm, and the Swedes thus a forest people. It used to be said that the forest was 'the poor man's coat', referring to all that was free for the taking there, the right of people to take and use firewood, berries and edible fungi. The Right of Public Access, that Swedish speciality and pride, is strongly associated with the forest. It expresses our ancient right to roam freely and take what the ground gives: windfall wood, lingonberries and chanterelles. The homeless fled there, where there was always asylum and the chance of survival. The late Bo Setterlind, unofficial poet laureate, has written an oft-quoted verse that begins: "Have you forgotten that the forest is your home? That the great, deep, quiet forest stands waiting for you as a friend?"

But the idea is a romantic one, just as the whole idea of the benign forest is romantic. In history, before timber mills, pulp mills and leisure-time needs, the forest was instead alien and threatening. It was not until forest clearing was possible that people could even live there; many Swedish place names have suffixes (*-rud, -ryd, -red, -röd and -rum* all indicate derivation from *röja*, to clear) that reveal the extent of clearance work; homes were built in openings, clearings and pockets in the forest.

The great forests were obstacles, they hid bandits and pawed creatures of prey, and folk were unwilling to go there. The forests of Kolmården and Tiveden in south-central Sweden were long the border between the lands of the ancient kingdoms of the Goths and the Sveas. Not until industrialisation, when the forests became a valuable resource filled with saw timber and pulp wood, did the concept of friendliness occur. Then the idea of the Right of Public Access took shape, as a kind of legal expression of the widespread 20th-century interest in nature: outdoor fitness, associations for promoting outdoor life, tourist clubs, the scouts, conservation groups and local folklore clubs. Sweden's Right of Public Access is no more ancient than this, which by no means makes it less valued or necessary.

Industrialisation not only changed the concept of the forest but also the forest itself, swiftly and radically. The romantic dream of the forest cottage was pitted against the crass need for timber; the modern story of the forest is an account of the disappearance of the forest. Because in actual fact, there is not so much forest left in Sweden. We face a paradox: there is adequate firewood and building timber, and regrowth is higher than perhaps it ever was, but there is beginning to be a scarcity of real forest. What we see is something else — more 'fir plantations' or 'pine-fields' than forest. Although it depends on how one defines things.

One summer morning many years ago, I cycled down through the forest to see cranes. My father had told me where to find them. Shortly after the Second World War, he had worked as a woodcutter for the Fuel Commission, and one afternoon he had approached a forest marsh and had been frightened by two huge birds that shrieked hideously and flapped around him.

It felt like an awful omen, and he retreated into the forest. He had no idea what the birds were but his workmate Harry thought they could be cranes, even though it was rare that they nested so far south, since they were mostly found in northern Sweden.

I propped up my bicycle against a fir and climbed up a rock-face. It was already quiveringly hot and the bog moss crackled underfoot. If I took a path due south, I would reach one end of the marsh. So I tried to keep the sun roughly on my left shoulder. A few willow-warblers were singing and buzzards mewed high in the sky but apart from them, the forest was silent and totally calm and I could hear my own pulse. It was a typical Småland forest, with pine-clad rocky hills and firs in the depressions, not especially dense — or 'well closed' in technical parlance — but quite varied and I counted up to eight different deciduous trees: birch, oak, ash, aspen, alder, hazel, sallow and buckthorn. On the hills were wild pansies, or night-and-day as we called them, and saxifrage. In the gloom of the firs glowed chickweed wintergreen and I came across some strands of twinflower.

Twenty years earlier, my father and his friend had felled trees here, although I saw scarcely a sign of it. There were of course stumps, half-rotten and covered with moss but the forest was, as forest, completely intact. They had been choosing their trees, 'selectioning', as it was called, taking only mature trees and leaving the rest for future growth. It was a cautious and flexible felling method, widely used in Sweden in the first half of the 20th century. I cannot remember ever seeing a clear-cut during my childhood and youth. After half an hour, I realised I had strayed too far west and was forced to trace a circular route back to reach the marsh from the south, with the sun on my back. There was a strong smell of wild rosemary and when I stepped on to the quaking marsh turf, I startled a snipe that crossly jumped to one side and dived back down among the sedge tussocks.

I had gone only a few metres into the marsh before I saw them: two large, grey birds disappearing into the forest darkness on silent, heavy wings. They were still there! It was surely the same two that had frightened my father; cranes can live to be more than

187

fifty and they pair for life. After a brief search, I found the empty nest. The young were probably crouched low in the sedge somewhere, hard to spot.

Cranes are very shy birds and very choosy about where they nest. It has to be somewhere isolated and undisturbed, ideally near large, grassy marshes or wet bogs, surrounded by deep coniferous forest. It was astonishing that the birds were still there, given the extensive forest clearing work done in the 1940s, and in the middle of their nesting season as well. The tree cutters had obviously worked very cautiously, felling only trees that had been marked and letting the forest survive. When the cranes returned, they could still recognise their safe old marsh.

In those days, talk was of stock-preservation felling; the idea was to create a suitable reserve in the forest — not too dense, not too sparse. The intention was naturally to increase growth; we are not to believe otherwise. Selectioning was not designed to accommodate cranes or grouse or woodpeckers — it was solely to increase yield. But selectioning had the happy effect of also helping cranes, grouse and woodpeckers.

'Ecology' was virtually unheard of, nor was 'biodiversity' even invented as a term, but the yield philosophy that guided forestry during the first half of the 20th century was without doubt better suited ecologically and better for diversity than the philosophy that dominated the latter half of the century — clear-cutting.

But there was a problem with selectioning: it did not provide the expected yield, especially in more northern areas. On the contrary, timber production stagnated and regrowth was at times sparse. And new times demanded more accountability.

In the '30s and '40s, there was a forest officer in Västerbotten province called Joel Wretlind. He was in charge of the state-run Forestry Company's lands and he had his own ideas. Instead of marking trees and culling in the way of the times, he turned to more radical methods: he clear-cut and burned off, clear-cut and burned off.

He was a man with his own agenda, prickly as a hedgehog, but he became a legend. Because he accomplished one thing: regrowth. Plants grew quicker on burned clear-cuts and grew better there than in enclosed forest. It was classic burn-beating, but instead of grain, he planted trees, either pine or fir. Wretlind's coniferous cultivation became the model for the new forestry policy. This was not only because of better yield; on the whole, clear-cutting was a more efficient, more modern harvest method as machinery roared into the forest: chain-saws, processors, skidders, logging trucks.

188

Clear-cutting spread southwards and by the '60s was established as the one true way. In the regulations promulgated in the forestry laws, clear-cutting was the only sanctioned method for 'final harvesting', as the term went. The selection system was, to all intents and purposes, banned.

Clear-cuts increased as did the total volume yield. At the beginning of the 1970s, 85 million cubic metres a year were harvested in Sweden. This was double the figure for the '40s and three times that from the beginning of the century. It was more than total regrowth and after a few bonus years, the pace was curtailed.

Clear-cutting is a violent encroachment on the forest, comparable to a disaster. Joel Wretlind based his approach on the forest fire: this was, he saw, a natural way for a forest to rejuvenate. Thus, he tried to emulate nature and consciously prompt catastrophe.

But final harvesting is a different and sometimes more profound operation than a forest fire: many trees survive a fire; fire scars, the vertical marks in the bark, bear witness to this. Besides, burning off was quickly stopped, as it turned out to be hard to contain the fires.

Forestry by clear-cutting changed the forest landscape irrevocably; one effect was that the number of elks increased enormously. This can be illustrated by the kill statistics: in 1940, 8,000 elks were shot; in 1960, the figure was 32,000 and in 1980, 132,000. Without exaggeration, it was an explosion of elk. Their swift growth between 1940 and 1960 can mainly be blamed on the retreat of domestic animals from the forests. Shepherds' huts disappeared and forest grazing was left to the elks. But the next eruption was caused by clear-cutting: elks were suddenly served dinner on a plate, and lots of it.

When forest is harvested and the ground bared, intense changes take place. The sun quickly burns off moss and lichens — if you have seen a stony clear-cut you know how the gneiss and granite shines — and blueberry, twinflower, chickweed wintergreen and everything that needs shade steals away, to be replaced by fireweed, grass and brush-wood. Decisively, at least for regrowth, is that large amounts of nitrogen are released when the trees go. In addition, there is more light, and vegetation grows fast and furious. Grasses do extremely well, as do all kinds of leafy brushwood, birch, aspen, sallow and rowan.

It was a feast for elks and a party for sportsmen. In the '70s, elk hunting became a mainstream passion; the hunt became the largest woodlands hike of our time with 300,000 huntsmen in the forests every autumn. But not everybody was pleased. Unfortunately, elks were munching more than grass and leaves; in winter, they attacked coniferous plantations as well, especially pine seedlings. Elks became one of the worst causes of damage for forestry and a difficult conflict arose: forest owners wanted to reduce the animals' numbers while the hunters wanted to keep them high. Since the adversaries were often the very same person — both forest owner and hunter — the outcome was uncertain. The quarrel has not subsided.

The forestry industry made its bed and had to lie in it. Clear-cuts were scientific and helped regrowth but also created an ecological contradiction that hurt the clear-cutters.

Naturally, when forest burns or trees are blown over by storms, reforestation takes place in a certain sequence. First, just as on a clear-cut, come grass and brushwood. The vanguard trees are birch and aspen and even pine, but firs appear later, preferably rooting in the shade of birches: it is said that the birch is wet-nurse to the fir. Only after a hundred years, when the deciduous trees die, can the firs build their dark world. Where pines flourish, the environment is less dark and more mixed.

But forestry had no time to wait for natural succession; the purpose of clear-cutting was to hasten reproduction of timber, so the natural life of plants had to be quickly and decisively interrupted. The birch was not longer wet-nurse to the fir but the enemy of fir plantations.

An enmity towards deciduous trees was born and in the '70s, it led to war.

Deciduous forests were attacked from ground and air; the weapons were chemical and mechanical — phenoxyacetic acids and clearing saws. The poisons aroused most notice and opposition. Crop dusters spread a mixture of phenoxyacetic acids known under the trade name Hormoslyr (a herbicide also known as 2,4,5-T containing mixtures of plant hormone mimicking compounds that upset the normal metabolism of plants). It made grass, herbs and deciduous trees choke on their own growth but spared coniferous trees.

No environmental battle in Sweden has aroused such bitter feelings as the fight over Hormoslyr. Directors of forestry companies sipped at glassfuls of the mixture on television to show how innocuous they believed it to be, and the head of the Swedish Environmental Protection Agency put his reputation on the line in claiming the poison had no serious side-effects.

But one summer in the mid-'70s, I met an old farmer in northern Värmland province. He lived on a clear-cut hill overlooking harvested forest areas. He had seen duster planes from a forestry company sweeping over the clear-cuts and went out to see what was going on.

"I found dead hares," he told me. "And dead birds. Once, fourteen birds in the same place. It seemed as if they had gathered to die. Nothing will make me believe that that poison was harmless."

Other strange accidents happened: game fish put out in ponds and lakes died; a few cows grazing on grass that had been dusted suddenly sickened and died; berry pickers who found themselves underneath crop dusters developed rashes and swellings and stinging in the eyes.

Worst was the incidence of birth defects and the conviction of the mothers that Hormoslyr was to blame. There was never solid proof, but much circumstantial evidence. There was a young family that moved to northern Värmland in the early '70s when 'back to the land' was the watchword; they were drawn to the countryside and the healthy environment it promised. They leased some land they believed to be in the middle of a forest, but a forestry company dominated the region and most was already clear-cut. Crop dusters had repeatedly bombed the brushwood on the clear-cuts.

The family was vegetarian and their diet consisted mainly of what grew around them. In spring, they ate nettle soup and dandelion salad. The young woman became pregnant.

"I didn't think about it much at the time," she told me years later, "but we found dandelions that were abnormally large and nettles that grew in spirals."

That winter, she gave birth to a daughter. The child had spina bifida, or spinal deformity, and was severely ill. Later, the couple heard that other women in the area had also given birth to children with genital defects. As she investigated, her suspicions grew that Hormoslyr was the root.

A bitter public debate ensued. On one side stood the forestry industry and, almost to a man, the scientific establishment. On the other, desperate mothers and worried people from forest districts. Opposition grew, the spark ignited a bushfire and some scientists began to research the chemicals. They made an unpleasant discovery: one of the components in Hormoslyr (the same chemical mix used by US forces in Vietnam under the name of Agent Orange) could be contaminated with dioxin, an extremely strong poison that could provoke cancer and harm the genetic make-up in humans.

In the mid-'70s, Hormoslyr was banned, and a few years later, crop dusting itself was banned over forests, thus ending the toxins war. Something unexpected then occurred: when the dusting was stopped, the need for poisons in forestry also abruptly ended, as though by magic. There was initial uproar and the forestry companies insisted they would imminently be choked by brushwood and die a horrible death by bankruptcy if herbicides were not reintroduced.

But when the ban was ratified, silence reigned. And since that day, no forest owners have ever demanded the reinstatement of toxins. Neither has any company gone bankrupt, certainly not for lack of Hormoslyr, Roundup, DDT or any of the other chemical weapons.

Perhaps they had begun to realise that the birch was in fact wet-nurse to the fir.

During the battles of the '70s, general criticism also arose over new forestry techniques. Clear-cuts had become ubiquitous and so large that it was impossible not to notice them. For many, it came as a shock that the old, familiar woods with their carpets of blueberries, special spots for chanterelles, stumps covered with twinflower and trees notched by woodpeckers seemed to have disappeared from one day to the next.

You couldn't even walk across the clear-cuts; twigs and junk timber covered the paths and you could no longer find your way. I often found myself lost in areas that I knew well and had even studied carefully. Neither did the situation improve with planting; pine or fir were set in arrow-straight lines and so close that after a few years, passage was almost impossible.

The old woods had become plantations. Instead of diversity of trees of different ages we had monoculture: the same type of tree and of the same age. Rationalisation, simplification and speed were the essence of the new age. When the techniques became familiar, it was even common to use cloned seedlings. This meant that not only was the same type of tree being planted across wide areas, it was actually the same tree.

In ecological terms, it was a gamble. Variation and diversity are natural safeguards against breakdown and catastrophe and the new, monocultural forest was no longer a forest in the accepted sense but a sort of cultivation, biologically as impoverished and monotonous as a field of grain. And the changes came quick and fast: at the speed that forests were clear-cut during the '60s, it was estimated that the entire Swedish forest surface area would be harvested and replanted within eighty years. By 2040 there would be no normal forest left, only pulp plantations and timber fields.

The outlook was frightening. But then a woodpecker flew through the Swedish forest, a white-backed woodpecker.

One late summer day in the mid-'80s, I was hiking through the woods near the lower reaches of the Dalälven River in south-central Sweden. The ground there is marshy, with lots of deciduous trees of different kinds, and well-known for its biodiversity. I knew the area as one of the last places in Sweden you could still hope to see a white-backed woodpecker.

It is a large bird, bigger even than the great spotted woodpecker, and with marked white stripes across its back. Easy to identify if you can find it.

It was common in the 19th century but was a fussy bird, and hard hit by modern forestry. In the classic handbook, *Birds of Sweden* by Erik Rosenberg, he wrote that the white-back is "actually a bird of ancient forests, still to be found, though rarely, in larger forests where there are still old aspens, rotted stumps and dying trees in stagnant swamps". Rosenberg proposed that "its stock and its haunts should be investigated without delay and measures taken to ensure the continued existence of the species in our ever-more cultivated forests".

The white-back is choosy about its food; it will not eat coniferous seeds like the great spotted, nor will it eat ants like the green woodpecker, but keeps to insects that live in wood. This means it depends on a supply of ageing, dead, rotten, decaying trees — everything that would be carefully swept up and discarded in rationally run forests.

I walked through a forest of thick-trunked pines with many fallen trees left lying across its slopes. It could have been a real, ancient forest with lots of lichen and moss-covered branches in varying stages of rot. There were even vintage aspens with thinning crowns and birches scarred by fungi. I focused my senses; it had to be here somewhere. And there it was! High up in a birch, like a splinter of bark, a white-backed woodpecker was hammering at the trunk, concentrated and persistent. Its red cap shone brightly, so it was a male. The white stripes were exposed with almost demonstrative openness. There was no doubt.

According to the description, the white-back is not an easily frightened bird, and it remained in place, picking insistently with its long beak at the same hole while I crept

193

around the birch for a closer look. It may seem strange, or at least unexpected, that such a typically ancient-forest denizen was not more nervous. But what frightens the white-back is not people but lack of food.

If the white-back is to be saved, much else must be saved as well. The entire forest. The bird must be able to find its special stag beetle grubs and it must have old, half-rotten aspens to live in. There is none of this in a field of fir.

It may seem an obvious and trivial deduction but the white-backed woodpecker flew through that Swedish forest as a revelation. In the early '90s, I was back in northern Värmland province again, this time as a guest of the forestry giant, Stora. A district forester showed me around, explaining as he did the new politics of forestry. Clear-cuts were no longer to be left bare: trees were saved in wet hollows and along edges, birches were left to seed and spread their sheltering branches, standing dead trees and old trunks were spared, and aspen and sallow were seen as helpmeets rather than enemies.

By a sweeping incline close to a road, he stopped and gestured expansively with his arm:

"This," he said, "I'm saving for the white-back."

It was a few hectares of deciduous-rich forest, with many tall, solid aspens, sallows, century-old birches and, of course, encroaching firs. It was almost ancient forest, and the forester was very proud; it was the ideal place for the white-backed woodpecker, or indeed, any woodpeckers. Of bird families, the woodpeckers have been hardest hit by scientific forestry techniques — black grouse, too, perhaps, and there are few places left for capercaillie to mate.

Something had happened. Only ten years previously, the forester's spared forest would have been seen as a crime. There was, namely, a clause in the Forestry Law stating that forest which, for various reasons, had become too thin or consisted of "unsuitable wood types" as it was put, should be "phased out for the establishment of new forest". In the preface to the law, promulgated in 1979, examples were cited of unsuitable forest: "overgrown pastureland; qualitatively inferior deciduous stock, often with several species which are judged unlikely to develop into valuable timber to a desirable extent; overgrown fields and grazing land; aged and extremely sparse forests . . ."

In other words, a ban on the white-back's forests. In the '80s, the Forestry Board launched an aggressive campaign to get rid of these inappropriate stands once and for all: landowners were called on to, without delay and within a maximum of ten years, phase out all disused pastureland, poor-quality deciduous forest, ageing forest and so on, and instead establish new, proper forests, that is, fir or pine.

It was like driving a chainsaw into the most vulnerable part of the Swedish soul, and the campaign ran dry almost before it had begun. Opposition was stiff, even among forestry owners; there had to be some limits to streamlining. Pastureland, slopes of juniper trees and deciduous copses could scarcely be called junk forest — this was taking product jargon too far. Swedish nursery rhymes and songs and stories are full of forest symbols. The burgeoning gloom of coniferous forestry threatened our common dream of happiness, and it was no accident that the revered author of children's books, Astrid Lindgren, led the protest against the Forestry Board and halted the campaign before too much damage was accomplished.

The fight became instead an alarm bell. About a decade later, in March 1993, I met representatives of the state forestry company, now called Domän, in Forest House in Stockholm. They were to present a new forestry policy, and suddenly, their tone was a different one. Now there was no more talk of valuable timber product in desirable quantities, rather of ecological bottom lines. And there was animated talk of biodiversity.

Deciduous forestry has a key role, explained the company's ecologists. And we must save old and dead trees and not harvest in wet hollows and leave trees around water courses and leave storm drains alone and shore up loose rocks and gravel on hills and save old sallow for lichen and old aspen for woodpeckers.

The white-backed woodpecker sailed through Forest House where people were explaining why clear-cuts could not be allowed to be bare, but should be adapted to nature; felling should be done so that species diversity is not threatened; shields should be erected on hills and slopes; marsh forest should be left untouched; paths should be left for animals and migrating plantlife and should anyone come upon mating grouse then they must tiptoe around the area so as not to disturb. There was no longer talk of marching through the forests, clear-cutting in box patterns, rather of creating gentler themes and variations.

This was how the new philosophy was expressed; selectioning was never mentioned but the word was left hanging in the air. Strategy had completed a 180-degree turn-around. What had happened? Much. But two things should be mentioned as decisive elements: one, the United Nations Earth Summit in Rio de Janeiro in 1992, when the watchword 'biodiversity' became a signpost for international environmental management, and two, the growing support for environmental issues.

People began placing environmental demands on what they bought in shops; paper had to be bleached without chlorine; timber was not to be sourced from threatened tree species. And when the German chapter of Greenpeace demanded an end to paper from trees harvested in clear-cuts and the rumour spread that Swedish clear-cutting was as brutal as the destruction of the Brazilian rainforest, panic broke out and the forestry industry hurried to polish its environmental profile.

But it was not for those reasons only. The turnaround was also based on a genuine insight into the ecological effects of clear-cut forestry. After a half-century of clear-cutting, there was not much ordinary forest left in the country — most was clear-cut or plantation, and many forest species, both flora and fauna, had found their way on to red 'endangered' lists. It was actually accurate, from the viewpoint of biodiversity, to talk about devastation.

The new, multi-variety forestry theme was embraced with true eagerness and enthusiasm, and it did not take long before you could really feel a lighter, softer touch in forestry. It was immediately proper to follow the natural order and allow birch and aspen to grow in clear-cuts and many forest owners were actually encouraged to invest in deciduous forestry.

One of my neighbours, on the other side of the lake from where I live in western Värmland province, had fought for years to maintain some old meadows. He was constantly at odds with the Forestry Board who thought the land would be better used for planting firs, and in voluble terms — even hinting that fines could be levied — called on him to permit forest growth. But he held on to his meadows stubbornly and persistently and cut and cleared, putting in birch, aspen, alder, juniper and a few pines.

Then, in the mid-'90s, he was suddenly being praised and was even granted a state subsidy for his achievement. People travelled up from the county administrative board to inspect the meadows. It was ideal, they pronounced, but ventured that he didn't have to cull so thoroughly. A few low-level bushes and brushwood are not a bad thing, they said, and go ahead and leave windfalls and old branches to rot on the ground.

There was a good chance, they explained, of the white-backed woodpecker moving in.

Tommy Hammarström

AN AUTUMN MORNING IN VÄRMLAND (p. 197). Light clouds of mist rise from the dark coniferous forest, like longing from a black heart. This is a landscape of tender sadness, the ancient home of the Swedish forest ethos, wilderness spoken by trolls and danced by elves.

THE MARSH AT KNUTHÖJDSMOSSEN (pp. 198—9). The bog is the eye of the forest and, reflected in the water, swamp pines and last year's grass find even better definition. The Bergslagen district is one of central Sweden's most remote areas and early on a May morning, you can hear the red-throated diver call under the moon.

A BEECH FOREST IN SKÅNE (opposite). It is spring and the leaves are still so young and tender that light filters down to the forest floor: shortly, leaves will thicken and shade will take over. Nothing grows under a beech and the ground is as bare as in the densest of coniferous forests. But there are riches: the beechnuts. They were once prized as hog feed, and farmland in Skåne province was appraised not for its timber but for the number of 'nut hogs' that could be raised; farms were described as having, for example, '116 nut hogs'. When nut grazing finished, beech forests lost their economic viability. It became more profitable to plant coniferous trees and pine and today, conifers dominate Skåne.

THE FOREST AT SÄRÖ IN HALLAND (p. 202–3). Wind-whipped, splashed with salt, pines stand on a stony slope over the North Atlantic. The coastal forest climate is both rugged and mild, and trees often grow old and imposing, although twisted to strange shapes. The distortion is mainly due to the salt: it sears the bark on the windward side, and the tree prefers to bud on the leeward, while its branches contort towards shelter.

THE LILLÅN RIVER VALLEY IN GÄSTRIKLAND (p. 204–5). Forest covers about half of Sweden's surface area, and farmland only seven per cent. This is how the countryside most often looks: forest both near and far, with a few lighter clearings in the valleys.

FIR PLANTATION IN SKÅNE (p. 206). Old beech forests are often replaced by coniferous plantations, as here on the Linderödsåsen Ridge. Fir grows quickly in the fertile soil of Skåne province, creating dense, dark forests, almost without ground cover. But the environment is sensitive as the roots cannot keep pace with the swift growth and Skåne's fir forests are vulnerable to storm winds.

BOULDERS WITH LICHEN (p. 207). A huge stone mound in the forest, garnished with silver-grey lichen. This is often a good indicator of forest health: lichens are both extremely durable and very sensitive as organisms; they can survive in the barren environment of a granite boulder but cannot stand polluted air. If the forest is clear-cut they quickly lose their foothold and the stones are washed clean.

MIXED FOREST IN ÄLVDALEN VALLEY (opposite). Autumn birches stand like glowing brushes on a slope of firs. This is no plantation but a natural, mixed forest of deciduous and coniferous trees. This is how central-Swedish forests looked long ago, before clearing and plantations made their breakthrough, bringing monocultural and age-identical forestry. The acreage of deciduous and mixed forests declined steadily in the 20th century, but towards the end, the trend reversed and forest of this kind, rich in birch, were strongly promoted.

THE INDALSÄLVEN RIVER (pp. 210—1). View southeast from Vättaberget Mountain in Medelpad province. This is an old signalling peak, with a beacon still at the top. A few scrawny but probably ancient pines cling to its slope — a biotope often described in industry terms as 'impediment' or useless land.

SUMMER NIGHT AT STORVINDELN LAKE (pp. 212—3). North of Sorsele, the Vindelälven River widens into a long, narrow lake, the Storvindeln. Lappland's landscape is scored with similar narrow lakes, or marshes as the local term goes: Storuman, Stora Lulevatten, Torneträsk. All belong to the large river system of the north. The Storvindeln is unique in not being dammed. The Vindelälven River is one of the four great northern rivers not tapped for hydropower.

FROST-BITTEN FOREST (pp. 214—5). It is December at the Österdalälven River and the firs are dressed in their first snow, the moist air from the rivers turning to hoarfrost on grass and branches. In the distance rise the mountaintops of Sweden's southernmost highland area, Transtrandsfjällen.

MOOSE IN A FIR PLANTATION IN VÄRMLAND (opposite). In modern forests, trees march in straight lines, all of the same species and age. The bull moose in a field of firs is also a symbol of modern forestry: this was recently a large clear-cut, and in the clearing frenzy of the 20th century's latter half, there was plentiful grazing for moose and over a few decades, their numbers rapidly multiplied.

219 FOREST

DRIFTWOOD BY THE UMEÄLVEN RIVER (p. 218). A birch tree on a rock has trapped a stack of tree trunks and branches at the Stornorrfors Rapids just outside the city of Umeå — a small reminder of the river's powerful transport capability. In the old days, timber was floated down almost all of Sweden's larger waterways, and logjams could build up to such a size that they had to be dynamited loose. At the beginning of the 20th century, there were 33,000 kilometres of timber floating routes. The last logs were floated down the Klarälven River in the 1990s. Today, all timber is carried overland, by road or rail.

A WOODPILE BY A DOOR IN LAPPLAND (p. 219). Before coal, oil and nuclear power, houses were heated and ovens fired by wood — all energy came from the forest. In Ammarnäs, birchwood is still a large supplier of household energy; it must be chopped and stacked in early summer so it will dry by winter.

SOMMEN LAKE IN ÖSTERGÖTLAND (pp. 220—1). Sweden is the land of a thousand lakes — in fact, there are 92,400 lakes of more than one hectare (100 times 100 metres). They are evenly spread from north to south, with only Skåne province and the central plains less blessed. Sommen, with its 123 square kilometres, is one of the larger lakes, and like most, it is girded by forest.

UNTOUCHED FOREST IN BERGSLAGEN (opposite). A few dozen kilometres north of the town of Nora is a forest of a few thousand hectares that has not been subjected to modern forestry methods: there are no clear-cuts, no plantations, no machine paths. It is not ancient forest; in the 19th century, there were mineshafts and smelting works and many people working here. But when the mines were abandoned, the forest was left alone for over a hundred years. So this is natural forest, a rare environment deserving of protection, and the Kindlaskogen Forest is indeed now a reserve.

HEAVEN HILL IN VÄSTMANLAND (p. 224). A gravel road through the woods, and a steep hill that ends in the sky, hence the name Himlabacken which means Heaven Hill. There is no forest in Sweden without roads. In fact, the network of roads serving forest machinery is dense, comprising over 200,000 kilometres. The average distance to a road is 480 metres — only a tenth of all forest area is more than a kilometre away from a road.

SNOWFALL IN A PINE FOREST (p. 225). A typical, March winter day in Uppland, north of Stockholm: driving slush through silent pines. It is dusk at midday and everything in the forest is crouching, biding time.

STORA SJÖFALLET NATIONAL PARK (pp. 226–7). According to the official dictionary of forestry terms, ancient forest is "old, untouched forest that has arisen through natural regrowth in untouched forest ground". This strict definition excludes all human impact and, going by this description, there is no real ancient forest at all in Sweden — all land has been impacted in some way. The Samis' reindeer have certainly grazed here and people have picked berries, chopped wood and hunted. But it has been touched only lightly and is as close as you will get to ancient forest in Sweden.

AKTSE FREEHOLD FARM IN LAPPLAND (opposite). By Lake Laitaure at the entrance to Sarek National Park, in the vast, mountain-foothill forest, is an old homestead, one of the northernmost and most isolated in the country. The first farmer arrived here in the 1850s and the land was then worked for about a hundred years. It is now a resting-place along the Kungsleden Trail, but every summer, the Swedish Society for Nature Conservation hosts a camp for people willing to help scythe the fields around the house to preserve the profusion of wildflowers.

FIR MARSH IN LAPPLAND (p. 230). Characteristic Northern Swedish landscape: thin, dark firs in wetlands. This is mountain foothills country, far above the official forest cultivation limit, a biological border for streamlined forestry designated by the Swedish Forest Service in the 1950s. This is not to be confused with the tree line or the Lappland border established in the 19th century as a limit for reindeer grazing.

CLEAR-CUT IN JÄMTLAND (p. 231). Clear-cutting has been the principle method of harvesting timber for the last half-century. 'New-growth areas', in the terminology of the forestry industry, are effective for planting new, practical forests. Most commonly, fir or pine is planted in tight rows, creating a forest that is more like a farmed field.

FOREST FIRE IN DALARNA PROVINCE (pp. 232–3). In the forest's natural state, fire and storm are the usual means of rejuvenation. Forest fires especially have a vital biological function. Recent discoveries indicate that efficient fire fighting can even exterminate some herbs and insects, and fires have been started specifically to save certain species. It used to be common to burn off clear-cuts to prepare for new growth. Here, a clear-cut fire has crept in among the trees.

MARSH FOREST IN DALSLAND (opposite). Forest that grows in wetlands is called marsh forest. It is a commonly occurring type, comprising almost a sixth of all productive forestland in Sweden. But it used to be even more common before forest ditches, draining and lowered water levels dried up many swampy areas, especially in southern Sweden. Its disappearance could seriously threaten biodiversity since marsh forest has many more species of flora and fauna than other areas. Here, birches grow in the water.

FETTJEÅN RIVER IN JÄMTLAND (p. 236). A silent, mossy rock, a shimmering waterfall, a dark eye of water and greying fir trees — the faery forest of Swedish hearts.

The Second World War embalmed Sweden's cities. I remember Stockholm at the time, and the other larger cities: Gothenburg, Malmö, Uppsala, Västerås. For the last time, sleds were heard jingling over streets paved with stone, yet to be asphalted. Old caretaker ladies jabbed at icicles on the pavements, and when in April slabs of caked snow could be shoved aside from the road, their underneaths would reveal horse manure, tram tickets and the pattern of the stone blocks.

I remember street musicians playing in courtyards, and recall throwing coins to them from the window. One had a dried shark: he had tied string between its razor teeth and played on it — this was the song of the city. It was before the time of code-locked entrances; front doors were locked at 9 p.m. and lifts in the better districts might have a sign saying: "Not to be used downward by service people". Kitchen entrances smelled of cabbage soup, water could be heard rushing through piping, sticky paper strips would fly when double-glazing was removed in spring.

The atrocious wave of urban renewal in the 1960s ruined many county seats and market towns. But a few decades later, some of the wounds have healed. Swedish towns, especially the largest ones, have become more fun. There are more neighbourhood restaurants, pavement cafés, theatres and clubs than ever; restrictions are fewer and nights longer.

You can still hear vegetable barrows rattle across market squares on Saturday mornings as before. Beer barrels chink on the back of a truck and music gushes from a hairdresser's. Dangerous industries such as the laundries, herring storehouses and train oil factories of the previous turn of the century have been shoved out. Water has been purified; you can swim in the centre of town in Stockholm, Malmö and Gothenburg.

On the slopes of the cove at Årstaviken, close to Stockholm's centre, the prim *kolonistugor* huts and allotments (originally leased to working class people with no other chance of weekends in the countryside) are like a fishing village in miniature. The last of the thawing snow is like industrial salt. Now is when the winter covering of twigs is lifted off perennials, the soil is turned, vegetables are sown and seed sachets are impaled on twigs. Melted snow makes black stripes along the cliffs of Stockholm's South Island. In the sun and water spring of the city, streetlights and neon advertising light up too early, and you notice the small lights because of the larger light surrounding them.

Church squares were the first public meeting places for discussing common issues. That was where public administration was born in the form of local householders' associations, marketplaces, and courts that resolved disputes and administered justice according to the town laws that succeeded laws of the land. Successively, Sweden saw the emergence of towns, then municipalities and then population centres. They were founded on the crests of hills, they bent around bays leeward of the wind, they jammed in under the defensive shadow of a cliff, they lined the banks of a river mouth. The city of Jönköping belongs to Lake Vättern; Karlstad is unthinkable without the Klarälven River. There is usually a hinterland with millstreams, forests for timber and fuel, fields and pastures to sustain households. In the 19th century, towns would grow up where a mine had been blasted as in Kiruna in the far north or where a canal had been excavated as in Motala (linking Lake Vättern with the Baltic via the Göta Canal), or even where rail had been laid in a straight line across the terrain.

The cities developed faster than the country as a whole. Goods were exchanged and coins were struck and expeditions were sent out. Workshops transformed into factories, inventions forced changes in lifestyles, new traditions formed new memories. The city became a source of energy not only through its industries, its gas domes, power stations and oil cisterns but also mentally and politically: the commonweal — the desire of people for agreements and pacts — was the condition preventing the streets from becoming trenches. The city demanded more mobility, more freedom; the guild system and monopolies were doomed to defeat. The cities renounced the fear that had built walls round the trading centre of Visby on Gotland Island and stockades around Stockholm and began expanding outwards instead of hunkering around palaces, courtyards and squares. The cities became places for discussion and conversation, for public art and buildings decorated to please the visitor. At the same time, associations, fraternal societies and brotherhoods limited the freedom of individuals.

Thus another ring encircled the city: knowledge, the thirst for news, democracy, the cross-fertilisation of ideas opened it to the world, attracting immigration and producing congestion. How would the city find room for all? How compact or sprawled should it be? How much may it change, how prudent must we be with our memories? Is spiritual confidence as important as increased material well-being? These are questions we must ask ourselves as Sweden's cities grow. Here we are in the information age, making us the nomads of free will. We must be careful not to be enslaved by the flood of information. In cafés, libraries, parks and clubs, access has never been greater. But we must assert our right to choose freely and not to have to follow trends.

Of course, the cities were living dangerously from the very beginning. New trade routes would cause some to fade away, as did Visby and Ronneby. Once important diocesan seats such as Sigtuna, just north of Stockholm, are now idylls beyond the freeways. Other towns were founded along the coasts or in archipelagos to protect the kingdom but were soon reduced to peacefully looking after holidaymakers. The rise of the landmass and shifts in fishing grounds made other towns such as Falsterbo and Skanör in the very south into retirement communities for golfers and senior citizens.

The capital might well dominate, but the smaller towns have their own cultural activities, often with a well-defined profile. These can be county seats such as Mariestad and Kristianstad, regimental towns such as Östersund and Halmstad, naval bases such as Karlskrona, university cities such as Lund and Umeå, industrial cities such as Norrköping and Västerås, cathedral cities such as Härnösand and Växjö. There are historic cities such as Visby and Sigtuna and towns which survived the renewal rage and which have largely wooden buildings in their centres: Eksjö, Hudiksvall, Öregrund. Around the First World War, almost three-quarters of Swedes lived in the countryside. Their hub was not the marketplace but the church green. This was where the school was; they prepared for their Confirmation in the vicarage, were vaccinated by the bell-ringer, went to meetings in the parish hall. Church duty meant that parishioners of all ages and professions met once a week. Not until 1862 would the parish be redefined as both a religious and a civil community and the vicar no longer be the automatic choice to head new councils.

The city arose to offer protection, warmth, and community. Behind its walls, one lived in safety; at its gates were guards. But city life a hundred and fifty years ago was nothing to write home about. The stench was strong. Stockholm was among the dirtiest cities in Europe. In the 1870s, goats and cows were herded to the doors of the middle classes in central Stockholm. What changed Stockholm, Gothenburg and Malmö were the railways, steamships and industry. A middle class arose that felt at home in the towns and cities and no longer fled to country manors as soon as there was sufficient money.

Even in my own time, I can remember farmers and fishermen travelling to town for market day (this was in Lidköping in the 1950s and '60s). They came with butter, chickens, game birds, burbot and vendace. Housewives with their shopping baskets would chat with the sellers; everyone knew everyone else, from the county governor to the brewery director, the air force colonel, the manager of the porcelain factory, down to the courthouse caretaker, the shoe shop assistant and the only Communist in the town council. By the square were the doctor's surgery, the bookshop and chemist's, two banks, a jeweller's shop and a haberdashery. Encamped in the ubiquitous People's Park were travelling theatre troupes, circuses and itinerant musicians. At the equally ubiquitous City Hotel, the blinds were drawn when Elsa, proprietor at the Thriftiness Bazaar, treated her family to a banquet; she feared the Baptist pastor would see the largesse and request a larger tithe. In smaller towns, you would enter most houses directly. The City Hotel is putting on a bridge evening, under framed Art Society artworks; it is Happy Hour at the Eagle Hotel. Teenage girls primp prior to making an entrance as the band strikes up at the Vesuvio Pizzeria on all-you-can-eat shrimp night. The veterinary surgeon supplies clear spirit to his punsch-drinking mates. The local ice hockey star passes by in his wheelchair. The diesel train reverses the points and departs, the ticket office no longer manned. The Kamrat bicycle shop, Ture's Drapery and the Hermes Transport Co. are standing by.

The mayor, the city planner and the district court's chief clerk visit the Masons one evening and the next are to be found at the town's haughtiest dining rooms, where Freemasonry is parodied. At the Friberg Rooms, a tailor is having a 70th birthday celebration with his brothers of the Black Eagle Brotherhood. The butcher and S, the former Nazi, the ironmonger, the brewer, the jeweller and his son the car salesman, the returning American Swede — you would meet them all at the Saturday morning market. There is always something new happening: for example, Chalky Anna has been mailing anonymous letters all over town.

Markets have been reborn. Farmers again drive in with goods. In the cities, immigrants have taken over with their chirpy, flattering calls. The impersonal mundanity of supermarket shopping is broken up by the human contact around the market stands.

A small town has waymarks, milestones for the memory and common symbols: the water tower, the courthouse, the hospital, the often obsolete army barracks, the bus station, the marketplace, the petrol station on the road into town, the market garden, a museum that — thanks to the local historical society — has moved from the school's basement to an old wooden building that had been threatened with demolition.

But in most small towns, the nucleus has been ripped out and replaced by cement rows housing department stores and municipal agencies, medical health centres and pharmacies. In Filipstad, west-central Sweden, for example, there is a proud row of wooden buildings facing the lake, but that is it. Arvika, also in the west-central forests, has kept so many old buildings that the sign saying Courthouse/Police Station/Tennis Centre points away from the centre, where the Tax Authority naturally also has one of the largest buildings.

District judges and bank managers are no longer paternalistic centres of attention; neither are ironmongers or booksellers. The new universities provide status and lively campuses but also a transient population; many young people merely pass through Luleå, Norrköping, Kalmar and Eskilstuna. On the other hand, the decentralised, virtual society seems to be giving small towns a renaissance.

Sweden has no metropolises. Even the town is a landscape. In 1978, when excavating an area in front of Riksdagshuset or Parliament House, passageways to history were uncovered and there were traces of a planted field from the 8th century. Even up until the 13th century, Lake Mälaren was a coastal bay with a fortified channel. Stockholmers of the time lived off nuts and sloe berries, chickens and geese, pike and cod, pigs and sheep. As late as 1612, the king used what is now the central Kungsträdgården park (literally: the king's garden) to grow his own red onions, cabbage and cumin; his gooseberries, cherries, apples and pears were brought to the palace just across the water in the Old Town. The garden is now Stockholm's most central plot, surrounded by banks, corporations and the Opera.

241

Stockholm's classical heritage is nature and water. When abroad and thinking of Stockholm, I see before me the hills, bays and trees. Stockholm is still the city of watercourses; it has no main street like Paris, St. Petersburg, New York or Barcelona.

Three archipelagos meet in Stockholm: the lake province of Mälaren, the densely built-up islands of the central district and the myriad of islands in Saltsjö, or Salt Sea, that carry us out to the open sea. Stockholm apparently has a total shore length of 155 kilometres. The cliffs are still there in the centre of Stockholm. The water has become so much clearer and cleaner as to be unbelievable for those who remember Riddarfjärden Bay thirty years ago. But the waterways have also become more crowded; traffic cleaves the heart of the city.

When Stockholm was founded in 1250, the sea surface was three and a half metres higher. The Ice Age was Stockholm's greatest architect. Many of the city's smooth stone slabs and huge ridges were destroyed by dynamite in the 1860s and when the differences in levels were evened out during the transformation of the city between 1955 and '65. There have been three periods of expansion for Stockholm: during the Great Power period of the early 17th century when the population quadrupled and the granges or urban estates were built on; during the industrialisation of the late 19th century that created a city of massive apartment blocks; and in the last decades of the 20th century when there was influx from the countryside and abroad.

But Stockholm is still characterised by its gravel ridges and moraine slopes, by its bays, inlets and waterways. The city breathes through its parks and the trees lining its streets. Fault scarps run in an enormous depression from east to west. Bronze Age waterways, now filled in, ran there, split into lakes and fractionated by points and isthmuses. It is easy to be stunned by the geological durability of the cliffs that constantly appear in Stockholm, by the powerful foundation stones, by the natural rock of the churches. This is a town with a foothold, although at the same time it floats on water. The rock is rugged, retaining both curves and edges until our own time, when it now corrodes from the chemistry of combustible petroleum.

Since 1950, eighty per cent of Swedes have moved away from their habitual environments. They have made fresh starts, and it has taken time to cement new relationships. In a TV-society with no elderly people, in suburbs where mud has petrified to concrete, relationships thinned out, families split and crime increased. Sweden became the

242

European country with the most apartment buildings. Between 1945 and 1990, the number of dwellings doubled. Half of all Swedes apparently live in buildings built after 1950. I suspect that it was not so much haste or lack of money that caused all this construction but more the desire of politicians to achieve consensus and conformity.

The big city succeeded the vast forest as a symbol of the unknown, the violent and dangerous, of murder, madness and rape. Sweden has not yet arrived at this. The metropolis, with its terrifying centre, is scarcely represented in our tree-rich cities. Stockholm, Gothenburg and Malmö are far from New York, Chicago, Milan or Madrid. Even the cement suburbs of the 1970s resemble, from May to October, a glowing garden idyll — reinforced by the marketplace commerce of immigrants who have updated our eating habits and given new colour to both outlying suburbs and inner city. The history of mankind is a history without cities. Gradually, in modern times, the city became a magnet, a temptation, offering change and development, while the countryside seemed conservative and stagnant. But even in ancient Rome, people were drawn to the simple country life; even then, people complained about stress and traffic noise, and sought out fresh air and clean water.

In 1900, every tenth Swede lived in a town; in 2000, every second Swede does. For most, the ideal landscape is another: sea and freedom, open vistas, summer holidays when life has a certain, specific weight. The city feels intrusive and stressful for many for whom the only solitude is in the car to and from work.

Town and country have always been contrasted. In town, people are venal and depraved. In nature, they are artless and pristine. In the country, people are at one with their surroundings; in the city, they are as anonymous as a morning in the metro. Farms are out of the way, shielded from view, even if the local store manager knows Everything. In the city, each building is a universe of slurred song, full of impulses, messages, quarrels, proclamations. Infamy and seduction are rife, laughter and assault, ecstasy and collapse, tolerant co-existence and deep stillness.

This contrast is oversimplified. Almost every city-dweller has his social network, his friends, relatives, contacts, even if without the daily scrutiny of farm society.

The city is the most constructed of environments. The city has magnificence and humiliation, great art and music, the worst degradation and the cruel exploitation of others' misfortune. For a city to function, its people must be imaginative and show solidarity; the city is an education in tolerance. In cities, people experiment with lifestyles. The young do it: graffiti artists, video arcades, skateboards and inlines; there are malls, the metro, festivals, meeting places, clubs. You find out which cafés are hot. You take charge of the city to create logic in your world.

A city should be renewed bit by bit, here and there, so that the changes are incorporated in the long term and a pattern remains, not immediately evident to the senses but gradually revealed by successive experiences. Block by block, we should feel that the city is cohesive, with a net of bus stops, meeting places, names that associate with each other ... An old city is a record of the flux of time and the imprint of history. When we demolish buildings we demolish history that can teach us about the present. In the 1970s, our city centres were torn down and reality was deprived of its streets and its legibility. The cross connections were annihilated, that fertile network so ambiguous and irritatingly difficult to map.

Let us take the inner-city district of Klara as an example. In one majestic gesture, buildings that had taken centuries to put together were torn down. Nine of every ten buildings were razed, hills and slopes with them. The mix of residential buildings, schools, hotels and workshops was erased; ancient networks were ripped apart.

Tiny and large lived close: the frame-maker, the bookbinder, the butcher. Old buildings with garret studios were cheek by jowl with rumbling newspaper printers where night became day. The Central Station was a cavernous shelter from the cold with trains thundering off into the dark. The worst of the concrete tyranny ended with the 1980s and imagination was given breathing space. The cause may have been a heightened feeling for history, for connections to the past, at the same time as decentralised flexibility in city planning succeeded the anonymous economy of scale.

Both brutality and friendliness have grown in my lifetime: shyness between people has disappeared and it is easier to make contact. Other things are eternal: the blue-black light above the yellow of streetlights on winter evenings along the quays, where spirits move stiff-toed. The newspaper deliverers at dawn, Lenten twigs with garish coloured plumes on sale in marketplaces before Easter, boat-owners scraping their vessels along the shoreline around the First of May, the summer night that clings tight to the eaves while the city sleeps with lights still on.

Our love for the city swings between passion and coolness, hard-won voluptuousness and frustrated dreaming. Sometimes we prefer to watch with half-closed eyes as life glides past, as though we're at a pavement café, from where we glimpse decision-making politicians and officials in rooms far above street level. We must nurture our ability to walk upright between the past and the future, so that we avoid condemnation by future progeny, as they who destroyed the Klara District are cursed now.

What is needed, in this time of unbelievable technical resources and an equally unbelievable ability to place the future in debt, is moral inventiveness, a creative attempt to do justice to the city's contradictions and the desires of its people. The private and the public, the planned and the random must be there, side by side, to create city spaces where people enjoy living and working.

Cities like Stockholm and Gothenburg have several hubs and each district has its own character. Obstacles can be more beneficial than throughways and can work to the advantage of meetings, small shops and events that might otherwise go unnoticed. Traffic that is too intense and central thoroughfares that are too large contribute to a weakened sense of reality and reduce the possibility of a meaningful life within a territory we can still manage.

Walking through a town with visible sediment from many epochs is an adventure. You are walking through history in the present. You are moving through a public sphere. At the same time, you cannot know if you are seen by anyone. Part of history is under the street stones or secretly stored in cellars and attics.

The reality of a big city is largely hidden. It brings to life man's old labyrinth dream. We walk into the unknown, searching, meeting the new. But we also have a need to chart our path, cover our retreat, and know where we are. Slowly, we make our city into a small town, a home, where we can anticipate what is around the next corner. But things are always happening; a house is torn down, a restaurant changes its name, blocks are broken up and change character. Sometimes I cannot find my way and sometimes I do not want to find my way. A living city is both a crime scene and a continuous cultural chronicle, a cellar niche to hide your notes in and a stage to parade on. With time, a city develops an inner reality which lasts, like a watermark, when the technological and economic edges are replaced by others.

That brutal wave of demolitions struck most of Sweden's towns; Stockholm was not alone. In the capital's central district alone, about 700 buildings — principally 18th and 19th century — disappeared. An old city culture was devastated: not only buildings but

245

also people were uprooted. If cities are to work better as arenas for different kinds of meetings between people, much will have to be changed, segregation ended, accessibility increased. But mass demolition, huge office complexes and parking towers were demonstrably the wrong method. Cities were deserted for long hours of the day. Plurality faded.

The 19th-century city of stone buildings, despised by the modernists, is currently seen as an ideal. The construction of an entire new district by the old harbour area in Hammarby is a convergence of the city and the archipelago. It is not a new suburb, rather a densely built district with a city atmosphere. Richard Sennett speaks of "narrative space": a series of parallel, occasionally contradictory episodes not subject to any single city planning concept but leaning on older, existing and new construction.

In the clear winter twilight, streetlights hover like illuminated glass floats. The sun gleams weakly, as did the tram lights of old. When dawn slowly arrives from the east, from the archipelago islets, it catches its breath for an instant, resting on its oars, then, with one stroke, it is here. Flocks of mergansers land in Ryssviken Bay in February, herons sweep over the reeds of Laduviken Bay.

Seagulls climb between the boat masts in Nybroviken Bay. A young woman heaves a baby carriage on to the quay while her husband swabs bird droppings from a deck. In all the comings and goings, a thrush throws a garland of song between the roofs.

There are always the cemeteries: at the churches named, in the Swedish way, for kings, queens or saints — Johannes, Adolf Fredrik, Maria, Hedvig and Ulrika Eleonora. Where people have been interred, trees flourish green. When hot air balloons, wheezing softly, glide over pre-summer rooftops, Stockholm becomes romantic and accessible and all aggressiveness and cold feelings are forgotten.

And if, under the stone, there is a landscape of tradition, memory and the strata of lineage, there is also a landscape that concrete and buildings have yet to conceal. This gives Stockholm its character and explains why the Stockholmer, unlike both Parisians and Romans, is no denizen of mason-built space.

Major cities must meet aggressively dichotomous demands: for quietness and reflection as well as swift transport; for order and for expeditions of chance — the unpredictable. What is homogenous, well planned and utopian is feared by modern cities. The voices within the walls and stone must be audible through the rumble. Everything must be discernible: agitators and orators, chamber music and rock, slapsticks and whispered love, the cry of sellers across Möllevångstorg Square in Malmö and the smoothed stone that tumbles into a chalked hopscotch square in a backyard along Stockholm's Rörstrandsgatan Street. More than others, architects shape our visible universe. Streets and buildings are thoughts and fantasies given concrete form by draughtsmen and builders. But for us who live there, these spaces are coloured by our perception and our memories. A street where one has been bullied or attacked in the dark will remain frightening even in daylight in later life.

The city is neither writing pad nor newspaper where news is eagerly awaited. It is an archive, gathering and documenting the experiences of centuries. It is more appealing worn-down than newly refurbished, with the thumbprints of past generations in its cemented surfaces. We can turn to Prague and Siena, Budapest and Bath to sense that we belong to a culture. Cities more than landscapes are shaped by events that occur in them, by books written about them. They are whispering galleries of stories. In Stockholm, the heights at Mosebacke, the principal road of Kungsgatan Street and Barnängen's lakeside perch are more than places and streets; they have acquired a mystical depth through those who have described them, lived there and borrowed their atmosphere. Cities are radiation sources, long hidden; generations that follow are zapped by leaks from the deep rock. In an ancient city, you can sense the previous lives as well as those concurrent with your own.

In English and French literature, memories relate to towns; in American and Swedish literature, to country settings. The city is more changeable than the country-side; thus streets and districts and their names and associations are filled with hidden meaning. Archaeological layers hide under your footsteps. You see them in perspective when you leave town for a while, when you have read the book through; that so many others have lived in the city and have also read the book makes you part of a larger consciousness, an imagined community where you can discover relationships.

The dark, strangely light-receptive brick of neo-Gothicism and the rough granite of National Romanticism unite in Art Nouveau, which dances in with rowanberry-garlanded hair and blueberry twigs, leaves rustling at its feet. Each statue and toothed frieze greets us from a culture with other limitations of vision than we have. These façades — on Vasagatan Street in Gothenburg or Strandvägen Road in Stockholm — move with the movement of the sun and the shifting shadows. Wilful dissonances clash with half-awakened echoes. The buildings are storages for the dreams of an epoch. For our ancestors at the end of the 19th century, the cities — when finally there was money enough to decorate them — were works of art in embryo. Our ancestors tore down Empire and Rococo — what they saw as old, inflammable wooden structures — to erect buildings that we long regarded as hideously pretentious and therefore, in our turn, often removed. But all that ornamentation was seldom superficial icing on the hard surface of pragmatism: it was emblems of justice, trade and shipping, science, architecture and art. These buildings often have a surface of fake efficiency, shown to the city to make it more enjoyable.

We experience the city based on impressions of things we met as children: odd door signs, front door handles, the tracks made by rain and the patterns of dust and dirt on walls, snakes, dolphins, open mouths of women, trumpeting angels. Memories linger on an Atlas with imposing thigh muscles, on plaster garlands in a yellow so pale they seemed to smell of vanilla. Memory rejects glass and large, flat surfaces; it craves detail, symbols, riddles and surprises.

The role of the building façade in the stage design of cities has increased in importance, since door codes and iron gates keep out far more casual visitors than burglars from buildings and backyards. How many stained glass Art Nouveau windows, how many cherubs on pale blue Tieopolo skies in entry halls have I not glimpsed without being able to approach? In backyards, carriage sheds and stables have been rebuilt into laundry rooms, studios and workshops. Stone and asphalt have been replaced by lawn and bushes so that children may play there and not wander out into traffic.

A good city is like a good façade: it is open to various interpretations, is full of feeling and makes you curious about what it hides. It takes us from repetition to surprise, from home to discovery. The city wants to demonstrate that people of diverse origins, habits and professions can tolerate each other and adapt to each other without surrendering either plurality or divergence.

He can be said to be a city's citizen who can exploit its possibilities, who knows its secret passages and short cuts and can interpret its bush telegraphese. He has to find benchmarks that counteract discomfort and alienation. The clearer, the more legible a city's symbols and seamarks are, the deeper the experience it can communicate. This means an integrated city, not one that is divided and fragmented.

We shape our cities, but at the same time, they shape us. There is an inherent, eternal, obtuse excitement. We never know whether we are ruler or ruled.

Per Wästberg

HORNSGATAN STREET IN STOCKHOLM (p. 249). Cities are shaped to fit cars: no other technical invention has had such comprehensive impact on the appearance and atmosphere of modern cities. In Stockholm, traffic sometimes gridlocks just like in a real global metropolis.

GOTHENBURG HARBOUR (pp. 250—1). With its half-million inhabitants, Gothenburg is Sweden's second city, but its first port. The city was founded in the early 17th century by King Gustavus Adolphus on swampland at the mouth of the Göta älv River and was long a completely cosmopolitan settlement, dominated by the Dutch, Germans, English and Scots. When steam power was developed in the 19th century, shipping and shipbuilding bloomed and by the mid-20th century, Gothenburg was one of the world's great shipbuilding cities. The days of harbour greatness are gone: all the shipyards have disappeared, as have many shipping companies. Today, Gothenburg is more of a car town, dominated by Volvo and its factories.

AUTUMN MIST OVER LIDINGÖ ISLAND (pp. 252—3). Mist hangs heavy over the villas of Lidingö, a suburb of Stockholm, only the high-rise blocks at Skärsätra pierce the cloud and aspire to become skyscrapers.

THE FYRISÅN RIVER IN UPPSALA (opposite). The building on the other side is the old university mill from the 1760s, now the Uppland Museum. Uppsala was once a ceremonial gathering place and commercial centre for the Svea nation, although at that time, the town lay further to the north, away from the river. It moved to its present site in the 13th century; there was a trading place here, where the Fyrisån River turns to join the commercially important Lake Mälaren. The first university in Scandinavia was founded in Uppsala in 1477 and student life still dominates the city.

MODERN CITY BLOCKS (p. 256). Residental district in Gävle, originally built in the 1950s to house hospital staff. The buildings are standardised and identical, planned with a ruler and a T square. Smart, clean and streamlined.

OLD CITY BLOCKS (p. 257) The streets in the centre of Ystad, in the far south, meander to a Middle-Age tune. The city has grown organically, with the 13th-century Church of St. Maria as its focal point. You can still find your way around with a map from 1753. Ystad has the best-preserved old town centre in Scandinavia.

RAPIDS IN NORRKÖPING (pp. 258–9). This is Sweden's first real industrial city, created by the Dutchman Louis De Geer in the 17th century with the help of immigrant Walloons. The city's textile industry boomed in the 19th century and Norrköping became 'Sweden's Manchester'. All industrial buildings were sited right by the Rapids of Motala ström, the major power source, right in the town centre. The industries have gone, leaving only buildings behind. The entire area has been designated a monument and serves as a museum.

ROOFTOPS IN VISBY ON GOTLAND ISLAND (opposite). The austere tower in the background is the Powder Tower, Visby's oldest building. It was built in the 12th century to protect the harbour and used to be known as the Tower of the Lamb. Once an important Hanseatic League trading centre, Visby had its period of greatness in the 13th century. The three and a half kilometre-long city wall, still in an amazing state of preservation, was built during that period. Of the city's seventeen churches, all but one are in ruins. Visby's climate is mild and the city is known in the florid tourist literature of our time as "the city of roses and ruins". The city wall and the buildings it encloses are now on the United Nations World Heritage List.

FRÅN GRUNDEN UPPFÖRD 1546

FAÇADES IN MALMÖ'S OLD TOWN (p. 262). The exteriors reflect an interior prosperity: this is a corner of Malmö's courthouse, built in 1546, when Malmö was still a prominent Danish city. Behind the courthouse is the 14th century St. Peter's Church, the city's oldest building, built in hanseatic brick gothic. When Sweden wrested the province of Skåne from the Danes in 1658, Malmö became peripheral and fell into decay. With industrialisation, however, Malmö began to grow and quickly became the country's third-largest city, famous for nurturing Sweden's labour movement. Today, Malmö has a quarter of a million inhabitants, and with the new Öresund Bridge, once again reaches out to Denmark.

THE GÖTEBORG MUSEUM OF ART (p. 263). At the top of Gothenburg's imposing Kungsportsaveny Avenue is the Museum of Art with its characteristic arches. In conjunction with the Gothenburg Exhibition of 1923, the city fathers built a complex of cultural buildings around a square, Götaplatsen. The architectural style was monumental: the purpose was to create a modern cultural centre and impress the world. The City Theatre and Concert Hall were completed in quick succession and the square became a true meeting place for Gothenburg's cultural cognoscenti.

THE FISHING VILLAGE AT FJÄLLBACKA (opposite). Houses cling to the rocky slope, clustering into a dense community of winding streets — a typical fishing village along the Bohuslän coast. In the mid-19th century, Fjällbacka was the most important fishing centre in the province. Today, it is a popular holiday resort and leisure craft crowd the harbour.

THE HARBOUR AT MARSTRAND (p. 266). Marstrand is an old port and fortress town. The Karlsten Fortress, once one of Europe's mightiest, was built at the end of the 17th century and closed in 1882. Marstrand was also a free port with full commercial and religious freedom and in the 18th century became a haven for the first Jews to settle in western Sweden. Later, Marstrand became a favoured seaside resort and had its glory days during the reign of Oscar II at the turn of the 20th century. Today, it is the fanciest place on the west coast for sailing.

PEDESTRIAN PRECINCT IN EKSJÖ (p. 267). A few Swedish towns escaped the 1960s craze for tearing down the old and building the new. These few still have old-fashioned centres with low buildings and stone-paved streets. Eksjö, an old garrison town in Småland province, is one of the most alluring, with a centre filled with wooden buildings that not only escaped the demolition fever of the 1960s, but also avoided destruction by fire for four hundred years.

HALLUNDA IN SOUTHERN STOCKHOLM (opposite). Row houses and high-rise blocks in one of Stockholm's southernmost suburbs. The district is called Botkyrka and expanded rapidly during the 1970s and '80s, becoming one of Sweden's most culturally mixed municipalities: a third of the residents have roots in a hundred other countries.

THE SKEPPSBRON QUAY IN THE OLD TOWN (pp. 270–1). A classic Stockholm panorama: the city seen from the sea. Yellow façades and white boats shine in the morning sun. To the right can be seen the stern lines of the Royal Palace, and in the foreground, a replica of an old firewood freighter, the Sofia Linnea.

HIGH-RISE OFFICES AT HÖTORGET (pp. 272–3). Stockholm's downtown area was modernised in the 1960s; the vision was of a city of light and space, unembellished and elegant. One of the city councillors responsible for the urban renewal programme described the five office buildings at Hötorget: "This townscape expresses creative power and belief in the future, with all the musical eloquence of great architecture. Five sweet chords, five trumpet blasts in a festival piece by Handel."

FAÇADES IN STOCKHOLM'S OLD TOWN (pp. 274–5). The Old Town is an island squeezed between the modern central business district and the heights of Söder, or the South Island. This is the original Stockholm, given its city charter in 1252. At that time, the lake to its west was only a bay and the Old Town was an archipelago island among many. Most of its buildings date from the 17th and 18th centuries although the many vaulted cellars are from the Middle Ages. The buildings seem to be leaning against each other, which they often are. On the eastern side, towards the Baltic, buildings are sinking into the clay and are slowly toppling.

KIRUNA IN THE FAR NORTH (opposite). In the Lappland wilderness, beside a mountain called Kieruna, meaning ptarmigan, a completely new town was founded by a royal decree dated 27 April 1900. What was possibly the world's largest deposit of iron ore had been discovered in the mountain and Kiruna quickly became Sweden's foremost mining community and northernmost municipality. To reinforce Kiruna's city status, high-rise apartment blocks were put up even in this region of cheap and plentiful land.

WINTER IN VÄSTERÅS (pp. 278–9). View from Djäkneberget Hill of snow-covered rooftops in Västerås. The name means 'western river-mouth', and signifies the spot where the Svartån River empties into Lake Mälaren, the huge lake delta that has historically been central Sweden's breadbasket and trading hub.

PILLARS OF SMOKE OVER BYSKE (p. 280). An icy winter day in the little coastal town of Byske in Västerbotten province. When the picture was taken, the thermometer was stuck at 33 below zero Celsius.

PHOTOGRAPHERS

INDEX

Page numbers in brackets refer to text